# Friendship, Love, and Trust in Renaissance Florence

*The Bernard Berenson Lectures on the Italian Renaissance*

SPONSORED BY VILLA I TATTI

HARVARD UNIVERSITY CENTER FOR

ITALIAN RENAISSANCE STUDIES

FLORENCE, ITALY

# Friendship, Love, and Trust in Renaissance Florence

DALE KENT

HARVARD UNIVERSITY PRESS

CAMBRIDGE, MASSACHUSETTS

LONDON, ENGLAND

2009

*Library of Congress Cataloging-in-Publication Data*

Kent, D. V. (Dale V.), 1942–
Friendship, love, and trust in Renaissance Florence / Dale Kent.
p.   cm.—
(The Bernard Berenson Lectures on the Italian Renaissance)
"Sponsored by Villa I Tatti, Harvard University Center
for Italian Renaissance Studies, Florence, Italy."
Includes bibliographical references and index.
ISBN 978-0-674-03137-1 (alk. paper)
1. Florence (Italy)—Social life and customs.
2. Renaissance—Italy—Florence.
3. Friendship—Italy—Florence—History.
4. Friendship—Political aspects—Italy—Florence.
5. Art, Renaissance—Italy—Florence—Themes, motives.
I. Title.
DG735.6.K458 2009
177'.62094551109024—dc22          2008026736

*For all my friends*

# Contents

# Illustrations

# *Preface*

I was truly delighted when I received Joseph Connors' invitation to deliver at Villa I Tatti in March 2007 the second group of a new series of lectures dedicated to its founder, Bernard Berenson. (The first group was given by my friend Edward Muir in 2006 and published by Harvard University Press in 2007 as *The Culture Wars of the Late Renaissance;* the third set of lectures was given in 2008 by my friend Charles Dempsey). I am grateful to Joe for his creative initiative, as Director of the Harvard Center for Italian Renaissance Studies at Villa I Tatti, in instituting the Berenson Lectures as a fresh and imaginative forum for the exchange of ideas. I also want to thank him for giving me the opportunity to reflect and distill my thoughts on a subject very near to my heart, and to share them with an audience that included so many distinguished and enthusiastic scholars of this field of studies, and so many friends, both old and new.

Joe envisaged the lecture series as an opportunity for scholars to offer a broad synthesis of a subject, raising some important questions of interpretation. There was no question in my mind of my subject being anything other than friendship. I have spent most of my scholarly life investigating the nature of personal relations in Renaissance Florence; how the ties created by kinship, marriage, and utilitarian friendship shaped the essential structures of this society, and were translated into political action and expressed in patronage of the arts.

Writing the Berenson Lectures gave me the opportunity for the first time to explore at length the affections that over many years of association with Renaissance Florentines, particularly through their personal letters, diaries, and chapbooks, I had seen flourishing within the framework of friendships often dismissed as purely instrumental, "mere patronage."

I owe a great deal at every point in my career to the professional support of colleagues who are also friends. Much of my pleasure in the study of history springs from the sharing of ideas and discoveries in the fellowship of friends working together in archives and libraries, at conferences and research institutions, and meeting, like the fifteenth-century Florentines with whom this book is concerned, over dinner tables in our homes and in "taverns," which appear to us rather less "ungodly" than they did to the subjects of our investigations.

I have met with my friends in such places all over the world; in Europe, to which our studies have drawn us; in the United States, where I have worked for the last twenty years; and increasingly, nowadays, in my native Australia which has become one of the centers for the exchange of ideas about Renaissance studies, from which it once seemed so distant.

It is impossible to acknowledge individually all those friends who contributed to the genesis of this book which, by its nature, is the product of a lifetime of research and discussion; to all of them I am more grateful than I can find words to say. I can thank by name those who, on hearing that I was working on a series of lectures on friendship, came forward with ideas and materials in an outpouring of interest and support. Among them were David Brown, Gene Brucker, Joseph Connors, Sabine Eiche, Richard Goldthwaite, Allen Grieco, Margaret Haines, Nicholas Eckstein, Jonathan Nelson, Brenda Preyer, Michael Rocke, Claire Richter Shearman, Janet Smith, Randolph Starn, Luke Syson, and Louis Waldman. The notes to this book also reflect my particular and continuing scholarly debt to the work of the first friend with whom I shared my interest in Renaissance Florence, Bill (F. W.) Kent.

My lectures were very much a product of I Tatti. Their form and content were essentially shaped over the six months that I spent there as a visiting professor from July to December 2006. I Tatti's library is an ideal place to review and reflect on the study of Renaissance Florence, and the community of scholars who gather at the villa constitutes an unparalleled human resource to aid in this. The friendship and stimulating conversation of the fellows and visiting professors of the fall semester kept me happy and excited about my project. As always at I Tatti, I enjoyed the benefit as well of the company of the many distinguished scholars who made brief visits in the course of my stay. Being in Florence gave me access not only to its archives and libraries but also the opportunity to consult more closely with the many friends and colleagues who live in that city.

I am extremely grateful for all the help I received from the members of I Tatti's staff, who took an interest in my project and generously put their expertise at my disposal, throughout my time as visiting professor, and during the ten hectic days in March when I flew back from California to deliver the lectures. I want especially to thank Gianni Trambusti for taking on the arduous task of preparing the slides for my lectures, and Fiorella Superbi and Giovanni Pagliarulo for help with the images for the lectures and for the book. Joe Connors was a constant source of encouragement, and I am grateful to him and to Francoise Connors for their friendship and hospitality, during the six months of my stay in the *podere* where they were my neighbors, and in March when I was their guest in the Villa. At that time I was introduced to my editor, Jennifer Snodgrass, who came from Boston to be present at the first two lectures. I greatly appreciate her interest and help in turning the lectures into the present book. I am grateful to the Andrew W. Mellon Scholarly Publications

Fund for support of the Berenson Lectures and for subsidizing the costs of photographs and permissions for this book.

This book is a product of I Tatti in the more profound sense that over the forty years since my first visit to the Villa under the wing of the supervisor of my doctoral dissertation at London University, Nicolai Rubinstein, and his wife, Ruth, I Tatti has been for me, as for so many others, the place to make contact; contact, through the books that it houses and the scholars whom it welcomes, with the world of the Florentine past that I have tried to inhabit. An I Tatti fellowship in the late 1970s and a visiting professorship in the early 1980s were lifelines extended to a would-be Renaissance scholar who felt herself marooned in the far Antipodes. At I Tatti, then under the direction of Craig Hugh Smyth, who became at once a friend and a patron, I was welcomed into an international "family" of scholars whose friendship has sustained me all over the world in succeeding years spent far from my original home and family. Cicero complained to his friend Atticus that "in all the multitude I cannot find one with whom I can make an unguarded joke or sigh familiarly." I have been far more fortunate.

*Friendship, Love, and Trust in
Renaissance Florence*

# *Introduction*

*Friendship, Love, and Trust in Renaissance Florence* explores an issue that preoccupied Florentines, as it had the ancient Greeks and Romans whose culture they admired and emulated: could the mutual affection and trust considered to characterize ideal friendship exist within the framework of patronage relationships, the functional friendships most men relied on to protect and support them when the state and its institutions were not strong enough to do so?

Forty years ago, when I first began studying the society of Renaissance Italy, I wondered why Florentines, wedded to the ideals of Roman republicanism, came, over the course of the fifteenth century, to accept the domination of the Medici family. Pursuing this question, I observed that citizens explained their behavior in social and political situations largely in terms of personal obligations owed to *parenti, vicini e amici* (relatives, neighbors, and friends)—those who naturally commanded their love and loyalty. An individual was en-twined from birth to death in a network of overlapping cir-cles of personal associates, beginning with kinsmen and ex-tending outward to include relatives by marriage, neighbors, and friends, whom his honor bound him to assist and pro-mote in all their endeavors.[1] The ethos of these groups—the ancestors of the modern Mafia as it operates in southern It-aly and was exported to Chicago and New York in the early years of the twentieth century—had precedents and roots in both antique and feudal societies, whose traditions shaped the social and political structures and ideals of Renaissance Italy.

As essentially honorary extensions of kinship, patronage networks clustered around powerful families, distinguished by their age, wealth, and civic influence. A response originally to a weak state, these bastions of private influence underlay and often subverted the government of elected officials. By the early 1420s, the Medici family presided over the larg-est and most influential patronage network in Florence. Its members advanced one another's interests in business and politics, which obsessed the merchant republic, since a share of public office or influence was necessary to amass and de-fend private fortunes. Through this process, the Medici cir-cle of associates was transformed into a partisan political group in whose hands effective political power became con-centrated. Thousands of private letters conserved in the Medici and other family archives contain pledges of alle-giance and pleas for assistance in procuring favors, such as lucrative and influential offices or crucial tax concessions for themselves or their friends, through the mediation of their patrons or other "friends of the friends"—a chain of mutual assistance familiar to us from the world of the Godfather movies.

However, in this city that led Western Europe in promoting the revival of classical learning and its integration with Christian wisdom, and where the cooperation of imaginative craftsmen and entrepreneurs created an outstanding commercial and cultural center, friendship had many other connotations. Florentines were deeply imbued with classical conceptions of friendship, both the highly idealized relationship celebrated in Cicero's *De Amicitia (On Friendship)* and Aristotle's vision of the positive powers of friendships arising among kin, neighbors, and other "natural" associates to bind together whole cities in amity. Christian conceptions of the friendship of God the Father and His Son, sacrificed to redeem mankind, and the brotherhood of men joined in devotion to them, drew vitality from the intense lay religious life of the city. Fellowship and camaraderie united artisans and artists working together to beautify churches to glorify God, and on patriotic schemes to embellish the city that Florentines considered the best possible place to live on earth. Affection flourished within all these forms of friendship, documented in personal letters, poems, memoirs, treatises, and works of art, only a handful of which can be presented in these pages.

Chapter 1 considers the many meanings of friendship to

men in this period, paying particular attention to important differences between modern and Renaissance understandings of this relationship. The vast interdisciplinary literature on the subject tends to assume that friendship is timeless and universal in its nature. And indeed Florentines, like us, read Cicero and Saint Augustine and recognized in their writings, as we do, a familiar experience. They understood the frustration of the Roman statesman, Cicero, writing to his friend Atticus, of gatherings that resemble many modern meetings or conventions: "My house is crammed in the morning, I go down to the forum surrounded by droves of friends, but in all the multitude I cannot find one with whom I can make an unguarded joke or sigh familiarly. That is why I am writing and longing for you, why I now fairly summon you home."[2] We know that Renaissance men identified with Augustine's grief at the death of a boyhood companion, as we do reading his *Confessions:* "Whatever I had shared with him, without him became sheer torment . . . I hated all places because he was not in them. They could not say, 'He will come soon,' as they used to do when he was alive and was absent."[3]

However, beyond the affections based on shared experience and interests, common to men in most eras, that are the main subject of Chapter 2, Florentines made very different assumptions than we do about the role of friendship in their lives. Scholars investigating friendship in past societies tend to begin with modern definitions, which represent friendship as a mutually intimate, loyal, and loving bond freely contracted between two autonomous individuals independent of family or other social ties and characterized by self-disclosure and the exchange of intimate information.[4] But friendship in Florence was not an alternative relationship to kinship, marriage, or patronage, and could not be clearly distinguished from these associations.

Indeed, friends and relations by marriage were embraced as honorary fathers, brothers, or sons, depending on the relative age and status of the parties, because the bond between kin was the strongest imaginable. The relationship between father and son was the most sacred of all, analogous to that of the divine Father and Son. As the humanist Marsilio Ficino observed, "The son is a mirror and image" of his father, that "second God" whose commands sons should fearfully and reverently obey.[5] "The dear, good, paternal image" of a father was the ultimate model for the guidance and protection sought in the friendship of patrons; thus Dante referred to Virgil, his patron and guide on his journey through the underworld, as his "sweet father," and the Roman poet addressed Dante as "my son." And when friends swore fidelity to one another, the most powerful promise they could make was to take on each other's friends and enemies "as if they were truly brothers."[6]

The beginnings of "authenticity" in friendship have been discerned in the Renaissance, when for the first time, "behind the social self, the bearer of roles and participant in communal action, there is another, deeper and more private self—one's real self."[7] I find no trace of this distinction in fifteenth-century Florentine sources; the Florentine self as presented even in private letters and diaries was always and necessarily a social one. To confine the definition of friendship to the exchange of intimacy and self-disclosure between individuals stripped bare of all other allegiances is to cut out the heart of Florentine feeling.

Similarly, the modern obsession with a search for "sincerity" in friendship and a determination to distinguish this from "rhetoric," with the intention of separating an element of personal feeling from politic or public friendship, is inappropriate to this small face-to-face society, whose members constantly crossed paths in the daily performance of a whole range of activities, both public and private; a revived classical rhetoric served in these meetings to constitute both personal and civil identities. Men's lives were dramas played out in the streets and other civic spaces.[8] The *Dramatis Personae,* following Chapter 3, enumerates the leading actors on the fifteenth-century Florentine scene and enables the reader to trace their appearances and reappearances from chapter to chapter as the themes of the book unfold, revealing how complexly and completely their interests and identities were entwined.

A modern insight that may be fruitfully applied to Renaissance social interactions is Erving Goffman's exploration of the use of strategies for the presentation of self, noting the social frames within which individuals negotiate to construct their identities. As Goffman recognized, in public situations personal feelings are inseparable from their social and political significance, since they must be communicated through rhetoric or by being "performed."[9] Many modern examples of this spring to mind: for example, former U.S. President Clinton was particularly adept at performing his personal feelings to positive political effect. When, at the funeral of his close friend Secretary of Commerce Ron Brown, he noticed a camera capturing him joking with another friend, his expression suddenly sobered, and he raised his hand to brush away a tear, who is to say (although many did) that his grief was ultimately less than sincere?

To most modern historians, patronage obtained from friends, interceding with friends of friends to help one another, equals graft or corruption and is incompatible with what they recognize as "true" or "sincere" friendship; thus, they are apt to dismiss many Renaissance friendships as "mere patronage." For Florentines, their relationships with patrons and the particular group of friends who depended upon them were an essential form of close friendship. As one man wrote to his Medici protector, "Please put me among the number of your very most intimate friends."[10]

Anthropologists and sociologists have a more sophisticated view of patronage, which they call "instrumental friendship," as a fundamental form of social organization required to facilitate action in many premodern or traditional societies. In recent decades, students of Renaissance Florence, previously inclined to view the city through the lens of its unique and often idealizing "high culture," have been led by scholars of the social sciences to recognize that Florence in this respect resembled many other societies, both extinct and extant, particularly those around the Mediterranean basin.[11]

This perspective has proved illuminating to students of Florentine society and politics, helping them to understand the importance of instrumental friendship from the Florentine point of view. However, as Felix Gilbert once observed, Renaissance Florence was neither a Mediterranean village nor a modern megalopolis.[12] As in other complex societies of the remote past, the rich and particular texture of Florentine relationships—what Leon Battista Alberti called the *filo e tessura* (the thread and fabric) of friendship, an apt metaphor in a city whose chief industry was the manufacture of high-quality woolen cloth—eludes the grasp of sociological formulas. For example, the social scientific model of patronage as a "dyadic" relationship, assuming its intrinsically unequal nature, cannot simply be applied to this society; the sheer number of remarkable men competing for influence within the ruling class meant that the most significant patronage relations frequently existed between social equals.[13]

Received sociological wisdom, perceiving "real friendship" as an exclusively modern phenomenon, relates its development to the rise of capitalism. The qualities of disinterestedness and intimacy are seen as peculiar to modern friendship "because individual bonds now occupy the space freed up by the emergence of the economic sphere governed by market relations."[14] This view highlights the difference in both business and friendship between the modern era and the Renaissance, when friendship and business were not animated by antithetical ideals, because friendship did not aspire to "forms of conduct profoundly different from those of the institutionalized social order."[15]

In economic practices, as in so many other ways, fifteenth-century Florence was a halfway house between the medieval and modern worlds. While business and economic historians often emphasize the modernity of Italian commerce, in view of innovations such as double entry bookkeeping and the letter of credit, ultimately, business was personal, and not primarily driven by the competitive spirit of modern capitalism. Success in business depended on the loyalty of trustworthy associates rather than on undercutting competitors in an open market; thus, as Richard Goldthwaite has observed, not even the Medici privileged making money over keeping friends.[16]

Just as business was governed by personal associations rather than market relations, what Florentines sought in friends was not so much intimacy as trust. This is apparent in Chapter 3, which considers outstanding examples of the testing and betrayal of trust and what they reveal about the essential expectations of friendship. Economic and business transactions—loans, partnerships, and credit—depended, like friendship, on trust *(fede, fiducia)*, and trust depended on the existence of personal ties between the parties. Florentines did business with relatives, neighbors, and friends rather than with strangers, and the loyalty of those with whom they wished to do business had first to be secured by forging some personal bond that had to be honored. Since a man's honor was arguably his most valuable commodity, trust was quite a reliable basis for business as well as friendship.[17]

The Medici bank was managed almost entirely by kinsmen, relatives, or close friends, such as the Martelli, Portinari, Sassetti, and Tornabuoni; most of these men were bound to Cosimo de' Medici by multiple ties of love and trust through marriage with his family and their closest friends. When his enemies exiled Cosimo de' Medici from Florence in 1433, they expected that his bank, the essential foundation of his power and authority, would fail and ruin him. To the contrary, the bank survived and flourished, which Cosimo attributed to his friends' determination to maintain its *fede*, the trust it commanded. He is reputed to have remarked: "The treasure of merchants is trust *(fede)*, and the greater the trust of the merchant, the richer he is"; an observation very similar to that of the legendary American banker J. P. Morgan, to whom Cosimo is often compared, that "power and money depend entirely on trust." It may be that business has changed less than some social analysts assume.[18]

When formulating a definition of friendship, scholars often proceed by a process of elimination or exclusion, not only of all other social relationships but particularly of any sort of instrumentality, any advantage or gain. Many Florentines shared the view expressed by Cicero in his definitive treatise *On Friendship* that an ideal friendship was one in which self-interest was of minimum importance, although it seemed to them, as it had to the Roman republican statesman, that in the real world of affairs, and especially those of the republic *(res publica)*, it was almost impossible to eliminate this factor.[19] Friendship, love, and trust were not defined by the absence of instrumentality; rather, instrumental relations required friendship, love, and trust in order to accomplish their functions. And while Florentines themselves sometimes perceived a conflict between the representation of friendship in accordance with classical and Christian ideals and their own quotidian experience, these ideals persisted as part of Florentines' reality, shaping their actions and perceptions.

For Florentines, friendship was framed by a variety of sometimes conflicting social, cultural, and rhetorical traditions. Chief of these were the classical, the Christian, and the civic. Having no language of its own, friendship used concepts borrowed from these traditions to define itself—as fictive kinship, as Christian *caritas,* as civic benevolence and *usanza* (propinquity). Friendship letters were also influenced by medieval rhetorical forms embedded in a feudal or courtly code, which described personal relations in terms of loyalty, fidelity, honor, service, and a love often teetering on the brink of the erotic. The "love and affection" owed to friends gained intensity by association with the topoi of romantic love, a longing to see and to serve the beloved, which was a staple theme of fifteenth-century popular poetry modeled on the sonnets of Dante and Petrarch.[20] Writers of letters of recommendation, by employing the language of religious observance, particularly that of the Scriptures, could remind patrons of their position in a hierarchy of patriarchs culminating in God the Father and of the divine virtues of mercy and charity; within this framework, obligations to friends become sacred duties and the reverence due to a patron akin to that owed to the Lord.

Within these frameworks, the differences between affective and utilitarian friendship are much less clear and of less importance than they appear to the modern sensibility; opportunities for personal feeling in patronage relationships were a matter of choice or chance. While writers of letters, which were the coin of patronage and the means of its cultivation, occasionally bemoaned the intrusion of utility upon affection, they did not insist on their separation. No Florentine could survive without "instrumental" friends or patrons, and most men accepted this fact.

So rather than following the usual practice of measuring friendship in Florence against abstract definitions based mainly on oppositions and exclusions, it seems preferable, as more than one distinguished scholar of the classical patrimony and its Renaissance heirs has recently exhorted us, to "only connect."[21] The range of *amicizia* in Renaissance Florence was vast, including utilitarian, companionable, erotic, and spiritual elements in a juxtaposition that seems to discomfort modern scholars but with which Renaissance men felt perfectly at home.[22] Fifteenth-century Florentine sources tell an inclusive story of friendship, incorporating a spectrum of related feelings in harmony with a predisposition to see this life and that of the next world as an intrinsic whole, as phenomena related by the models of essential relationships. Friendship was an extension of patriarchal kinship, linking heaven and earth in the personae of the patriarchal patron and God the Father.

"Heavenly friendship" has not figured in most scholarly

discussions of Renaissance friendship, despite the fact that the cult of the saints, men's "very special friends" and advocates in heaven, is a vivid expression of an essential connection in the minds of Florentine Christians between friendship and patronage.[23] Nor have the visual texts familiar to art historians been generally integrated into discussions of Renaissance friendship. With both these innovations, my aim is to recreate the very particular contexts of fifteenth-century experience, to understand Florentines, as far as is possible from their own point of view.

This explains an omission that may strike the modern reader as odd. I have said very little about women in these chapters. This is partly because of the limited time frame of the original lectures, and partly because in Florence, one of the most patriarchal societies of fifteenth-century Europe, friendship was seen as a male prerogative and pleasure. Women, regarded as imperfect, were not considered capable of ideal friendship. Nor did they possess a public role in the intensely civic world that was the essential context of male friendships. Consequently, they also had a very restricted role in the creation of record. There is, however, rich evidence of friendships not only among women but also between women and men in the sixteenth century. The relation between Michelangelo and Vittoria Colonna, briefly considered at the conclusion of Chapter 3, is one such example that has been extensively explored by other scholars. Similarly interesting examples of women's friendships are attracting increasing attention.[24]

The relationships examined in the following chapters, especially in Chapter 3, show how fine was the line between friendship and enmity, between love and hatred in Renaissance Florence. Friendship, love, and trust cannot be properly understood without reference to their obverse; however, issues such as the nature and sources of the acute tensions in Florentine society are beyond the small scope of this book. Moreover, they have already been vigorously addressed by many writers, beginning most notably with Dante, whose *Inferno* is filled with factious Florentines who were tearing their city apart.[25] It may seem rather bold, indeed foolhardy, to address in three short lectures, only slightly expanded for publication, such an immensely complex issue as the nature of friendship, so extensively discussed and hotly debated by sociologists, anthropologists, and historians. What I hope to offer here is not a conclusive definition or description of Florentine friendship, in any of its many senses, but rather a brief introduction to a variety of fifteenth-century perspectives on this relationship.

ONE

*What Did Friendship Mean?*

On October 22, 1441, a competition for the best popular poem on the subject of friendship, organized by the brilliant humanist and architect Leon Battista Alberti, and sponsored by Piero de' Medici, elder son of Florence's leading citizen and patron, Cosimo de' Medici, was held in the cathedral, Santa Maria del Fiore (Figure 1.1). Events of major significance to Florentines, civic as well as religious, were accommodated within its enormous space, under Filippo Brunelleschi's newly completed cupola, which to Alberti (Figure 1.2) seemed "vast enough to cover the entire Tuscan population with its shadow." Men "of every rank," described as "the whole of the city of Florence," gathered to listen to the recital of eight lengthy entries describing friendship *(amicizia)* in a contest called the "certame coronario" in imitation of similar competitions held in ancient Rome.[1]

Almost all the participants took as their point of departure the classical debate on friendship, most memorably and accessibly presented by the Roman republican statesman and writer Marcus Tullius Cicero. In his *De Amicitia,* Cicero argued that while the term "friendship" commonly referred to relations involving three main elements or motives—profit, pleasure and virtue—only the love of virtuous men indifferent to gain could be considered true or ideal friendship, and this relation was rare.[2] At the *certame coronario,* the learned cleric Leonardo Dati considered that proposition and observed that men of every Florentine estate and rank were disabled in some way from forging true friendships: patricians by envy and calumny, the fortunate rich by ambition and indulgence, merchants by avarice and suspicion, the vulgar by ignorance, and scholars by poverty and hypocrisy.[3]

Anselmo Calderoni, herald and entertainer to the Signoria, the city's governing magistracy, appealed to Cicero's authority in stressing the importance of the underlying motive for making friends. Honor and profit are benefits that flow naturally from the association of the virtuous, but friendship should be *contracted* in pure love.

> I begin with Tulio . . . he would say that friendship
>    exists only
> when with the purest good faith
> one loves another with profit and honor

1.1. Cathedral of Florence (Santa Maria del Fiore).

1.2. Leon Battista Alberti, *Self-portrait,* bronze plaque.

and one is like the other, without vice,
never separated in joy or in sorrow; this is his gist.
So he says that a friend who appears to contract
a friendship solely for his own ends *(per trarre alle sue gueffe),*
is a travesty of a friend *(questo è amico da beffe).*[4]

The discussion based on the classical Ciceronian definition of friendship tended to dead end in the conclusion that
true friendship was almost impossible to achieve. Renaissance
Florentines, however, had a way out of the impasse unavail-
able to the men of antiquity. There was one ideal friend, and
He was God, or his son, Jesus Christ. Mariotto Davanzati, a
distinguished patrician poet, declared His mercy to be the
true function of *amicizia:*

> A friend helps us . . . by bearing the punishment for our
>   faults
> as the Majesty serene created Love
> and the angels, and arranged for man
> to make Mary full of grace,
> for our sins: . . . and to expiate such crimes
> put his Son on the cross as our friend.[5]

In keeping with his plebeian origins and his profession
as an entertainer, the herald Calderoni had begun his recita-
tion with a self-deprecating joke: "I know that among the
dates, the fig must be my fruit." But he continued in high se-
riousness:

> I say that we are made of flesh and bone
> and frail, turning like the leaves

> as the whim strikes us,
> sometimes for desire and sometimes for disdain,
> and anger deprives us of the capacity for virtue,
> and turns us to vice, more's the pity,
> and strips friendship bare,
> and creates hatred unworthy of heaven.

Of all friends, he said:

> the truest I would say, without a doubt,
> is Almighty God,
> who is truly loving to all his friends
> . . . I conclude in effect
> that the friendship of God is perfect,
> and never false; and yes, all else is partisanship
> *(ogn'altra [è] setta)*.[6]

The nature of friendship had long been a favorite subject
for reflection in the private diaries and chapbooks *(zibaldoni)*
particular to the Florentine tradition of record keeping. These
had evolved from commercial account books and records of
political office holding to include familial histories and literary texts, serving as compilations of experience and wisdom
for the benefit of descendants. The *certame coronario* brought
friendship to the very forefront of Florentines' attention. Alberti boasted that "already within ten days more than ten
times twenty copies of the entire contest were transcribed,
and flew around Italy to all the princes, and were requested
by all educated men, praised by all worthy ones."[7]

Compilers of *zibaldoni*, intended for the owner's "pleasure and profit" *(diletto et utilitade)*, or dedicated to "all my friends," prefaced the poems with eyewitness accounts of the contest. Several suggested that the recitations begun in the cathedral on October 22 continued for a second day and that verses were performed elsewhere that week. Certainly, the corpus of poems associated with the contest is much larger than the number of those actually recited, and over the following decades a steady stream of poets aired their reflections on the subject of friendship.[8]

The contributions to the *certame coronario* of 1441 dramatize an essential enterprise of early Renaissance Florentines: to integrate and reconcile classical writings with Christian wisdom and to apply the insights of both cultural traditions to real issues arising in the daily life of their city. By the early fifteenth century, ancient Roman writings—Quintilian's handbook on the orator's education *(Institutiones oratoriae)* and Cicero's *Orator* and *On Oratory*—were added to vernacular proverbs and clerical injunctions as authorities on social behavior, including friendship. Many *zibaldoni* contained aphorisms and summaries of the arguments of these authors, and quite a few Florentines owned complete copies of Cicero's writings. Of three dozen volumes in the library of the statesman Dietisalvi Neroni, whose defection from the ranks of Medici friends will be discussed in Chapter 3, nine were works of Cicero, including a copy of *De Amicitia*, which he lent to his brother Giovanni.[9]

Leon Battista Alberti was the illegitimate son of an old and distinguished family exiled from Florence in 1401 for its

opposition to the prevailing political regime. After a humanist education and studies in law at the University of Bologna,
he spent the early years of his professional life working for
the bureaucracy attached to the papal court. In 1428 the Florentine government lifted the ban of exile against the Alberti, and in the mid-1430s, Leon Battista moved with Pope
Eugenius IV to Florence. Alberti's own contribution to the
*certame coronario* was a short and mordant verse suggesting
that *amicizia* dwelt in heaven and seldom descended to earth
for fear of the envy that was her evil enemy. Envy was also
a major theme of the recorded *obiter dicta* of Cosimo de'
Medici; in 1433 he too was exiled by his political opponents
but repatriated only a year later when his fellow Florentines
acknowledged that his enormous wealth and decisive leadership were indispensable to the city's welfare.[10]

In the fourth book of his treatise *Della Famiglia (On the
Family)*, written in 1434 and entitled "On Friendship," Alberti
offered a critical reassessment of Cicero's characterization of
friendship in the light of his own experience. Although much
of what he said accorded with popular wisdom expressed in
the *ricordi* or diaries of merchants like Giovanni Morelli and
Paolo di Messer Pace da Certaldo, Alberti's view of friendship also reflects his personal experience, which had been
particularly harsh.[11] Clearly, he felt estranged from his native
land, abandoned by his family, and unsuccessful in obtaining
aid from expected allies at the courts he had served. After his
return to Florence, Alberti turned increasingly to friends
of choice from humanist and artistic circles. These included

the group of groundbreaking artists whose achievements he praised in dedicating his treatise *On Painting* to the architect Brunelleschi, singling out "our great friend the sculptor Donatello . . . and the others," the sculptors Lorenzo Ghiberti and Luca della Robbia, and the painter Masaccio.[12]

In his description of friendship, Alberti emphasized the tension between learning and experience and between virtue, pleasure, and utility as bases for friendship. He presented friendship as a defensive strategy for survival in a world "so full of diverse talents, differences of opinion, such uncertainty of desire, perversity of customs, ambiguity, variety and obscurity of judgments, with such an abundance of fraudulent, false, perfidious, bold, audacious and rapacious men . . . [that] one has to be far-seeing, alert, and cautious in the face of fraud, traps and betrayals . . . one must oppose these with constancy, moderation, and inner strength. I would want to be expert in these matters any man with whom I hoped to forge a friendship and profit from it." This passage represents a beleaguered vision, and a not uncommon one, of friendship in the world of Cosimo de' Medici and his friends—and enemies.[13]

In the wake of Petrarch's intense personal admiration in the 1340s and 1350s for the Roman republican statesman and orator, Cicero became the classical hero of the early Florentine Renaissance. Aristotle was scarcely mentioned at the *certame coronario*, although his *Politics* were well known and his *Ethics* had been available to Florentines since 1416 in a translation by Leonardo Bruni, the city's humanist chancellor and leading publicist of Florentine republicanism. In fact, Aristotle's view that the perfect friendship is between the good, and those who resemble each other in virtue, but that relationships based on pleasure and utility—however contingent and transient, however unequal the status of the parties and the benefits offered and received—are nevertheless friendships, accords much more closely with Florentine reality than Cicero's idealized demands of this relationship (Figure 1.3).[14]

Aristotle's view of the civic uses of friendship, popularized by Dante and his contemporaries at the turn of the thirteenth and fourteenth centuries, had been an essential foundation of the ethos of the early commune, which drew heavily on the example of the Greek polis as the ideal political unit, emphasizing cooperation for the common good, which was also "the good of the commune."[15] Dante remained high on the list of fifteenth-century best-selling authors, and in the 1440s these ideas took on fresh life in Matteo Palmieri's immensely influential treatise *On Civic Life*, cited by the banker Giovanni Rucellai in his *zibaldone*, and quoted verbatim in the letters of other leading citizens, including Agnolo Acciaiuoli.[16]

In Palmieri's work, Rome's experience is made to exemplify the discord that results when citizens cease to base the unity of the commune on the friendship of its citizens. These are bound together in amity through the natural extension of large families, "who, giving and receiving in legitimate marriages relatives and love, come to constitute a good part of the city, affectionately bound by ties of marriage *(parentela)*,

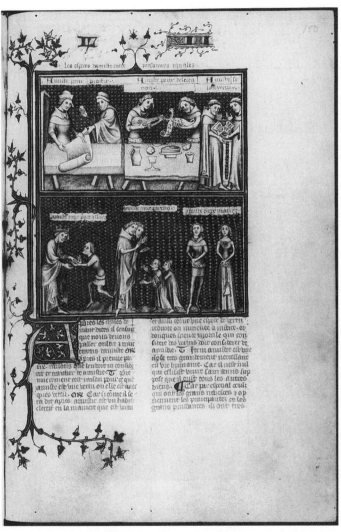

1.3. The *Ethics* of Aristotle, fourteenth-century French manuscript, representing the varieties of friendship: *Friendship for profit, friendship for pleasure, virtuous friendship, friendship between prince and subject, friendship between relatives, and friendship between spouses.*

supporting one another, and among themselves renewing advice, favors and aid, which bring enhanced capacities and abundant fruit to our lives." To this group of friends, already "a good part of the city," are added friendships that are "even closer" than the associations of relatives, because "good-will and love" cannot be taken away from friendship; thus, in the end, "friendship is the sole link that binds cities together."[17]

The poem presented at the *certame coronario* by Francesco d'Altobianco degli Alberti, a kinsman of Leon Battista whose life also exemplified the misfortunes of their lineage, shows the continuing influence of these views, presenting utilitarian friendship in a positive light provided that it operated within the judicious context of faith and religion.

> The profitable element of friendship is praised, welcomed and
>   happily enjoyed;
> it is delightful and necessary among mortals
> that honest requests be fully granted,
> and the principal qualities that it includes
> are generosity, munificence and beneficence (*grazia, munificenzia*
>   *e benefizio*).
> Each of these has its proper function; along with truth,
>   trustworthiness *(fede)* and religion, which maintain our
>   good judgment.[18]

An Aristotelian conception of friendship as a more discriminating refinement of other natural charitable and supportive social bonds, such as kinship, operating in a Christian framework where earthly friendships were seen as analogous

to the divine, helped in Renaissance eyes to elevate the friendships of patronage networks above the political context in
which Cicero's contemporaries had placed them, as do most
modern scholars.[19]

~~~

The remainder of this chapter explores more fully the aspects of friendship seen by the participants of the *certame
coronario* as most significant. Chief of these was the "heavenly
friendship" of God the Father and His Son, mediated, as
earthly patrons mediated between their friends, by the intercession of the saints, men's "very special friends" and patrons
in heaven.[20]

The essence of Renaissance friendship, whether it entailed
profit or not, was the obligation to assist one's friend in all
his enterprises and to marshal the resources of the entire
friendship circle or patronage network—all the friends of
the friends—to intercede with others on his behalf. The elements of mutual obligation and intercession common to
friends, patrons, and saints helped to fuse their roles in Florentine minds, as they had done for Christians since late
antiquity. The concepts and structures of patronage that
shaped Florentine society in turn informed its members' understanding of a *religio amicitiae*. Relationships between patrons and clients served as the model on which perceptions
of heavenly friends were based. Ser Paolo di Ser Pace da
Certaldo saw heaven as a celestial court peopled by patron
saints whom he described in the language of personal pa-

tronage as *avvocati*, advocates or intermediaries with God, defending the interests of the pious, their clients and friends or *raccomandati*—those whose interests they recommended to others. For Paolo, the search for salvation was a search for divine patronage.[21]

Thus, although they might not immediately appear as such, images of Christ, the Virgin, and the saints are images of friendship. The link between earthly patrons and patron saints was made explicit in images like Fra Angelico's altarpiece (Figure 1.4) for the high altar of the church of the convent of San Marco. Commissioned by Cosimo de' Medici in the early 1440s as part of his renovation of this Dominican house in the neighborhood of the Medici palace, the painting articulates the association between Florentine conceptions of the right ordering of this world and that of the next, between friendship, patronage, and salvation. Just as the earthly patron/friend, whom Cosimo embodied par excellence, provided patriarchal protection and justice for his clients/friends in return for their loyalty and support, in return for his devotion and charity to the church and its poor Cosimo's patron saints, Cosmas and Damian, similarly protected and interceded for him before God, the supreme Father and judge.

Not long before Fra Angelico began this work, Alberti had suggested in his treatise *On Painting* that the artist include someone "who tells the spectators what is going on, . . . beckons them with his hand to look."[22] Here it is Saint Cosmas who mediates between the convocation of saints in heaven and the viewer outside the picture plane, whom he addresses with his gaze as he gestures toward the Virgin and Child. Patron and mediator in heaven, as Cosimo was on earth, Saint Cosmas was Cosimo's direct link to the supreme intercessors, the Virgin and Christ. Directly in the Virgin's line of vision, Damian, name saint of Cosimo's twin brother who died in infancy, balances Cosmas in the foreground: he looks at the Virgin, his back to the viewer. Florentines, attuned to the weight of geometric shapes in calibrating meaning by other images of mediation and intercession, such as Masaccio's *Trinity* (Figure 1.5) and the older *Trinity* in the cathedral (Figure 1.6), would have noticed that the figures of Cosmas and Damian literally support the composition, as their devotees did the convent, forming the base of a triangle whose apex is a classical triumphal arch—similar to the one in Masaccio's *Trinity*—crowning the Virgin's throne.

Fra Angelico depicts in the San Marco altarpiece a chain of intercession linking heaven and earth, of associations that range, uninterrupted, from the power of Medici patrons to dispense charity and liberality to their friends in the convent and the community it served, to an assertion of their direct connection with their saintly patrons and friends, intercessors soliciting the liberality of the Virgin in the hope of their own salvation, and that of all the altarpiece's Florentine viewers.

This perceived connection was dramatized on the occasion of the consecration of Florence's cathedral after the completion of Brunelleschi's cupola in 1436. The ceremonies

1.4. Fra Angelico, *Virgin and Child with Saints Cosmas and Damian,* altarpiece commissioned by Cosimo de' Medici for the convent of San Marco.

1.5. Masaccio, *Trinity*, fresco, Santa Maria Novella, Florence.

1.6. Lorenzo Monaco, attributed, *The Intercession of Christ and the Virgin,* in the fifteenth century in the Cathedral of Florence.

offered several variations on the theme of mercy and intercession. First the city's governing magistracy made it known
that they had liberated a number of prisoners, a concession
that paralleled the pope's charitable granting of indulgences
on this special occasion to hasten the liberation of souls
from purgatory, which ultimately evoked Christ's liberation
of souls from hell on the day of the Last Judgment. At the
conclusion of the mass, the cardinal of San Marcello an-
nounced the number of indulgences for attendance at this
ceremony as six; then, as the clerical chronicler recorded,
"encouraged by the pleas of the noble citizen Cosimo de'
Medici, he altered that to seven." Cosimo continued to plead
for an increase in the treasury of merit upon which Florentines might draw for their salvation, and the bargaining
ended with the cardinal's agreeing to ten, "having already refused this to all the other cardinals and lords of Florence."[23]

This public, and undoubtedly staged, demonstration of
Cosimo's power as an intercessor for the Florentine people
figured prominently in popular descriptions of the event.
Cosimo's intervention was seen to link him to a chain of intercessors culminating in the Virgin herself. It was this "mar-
vellous charity," the spiritual face of his secular patronage
that, according to the shoemaker poet Giovanni di Cino,
made him "worthy of immortality" and the title of "father
of his country" in a higher sense than could his worldly
power and patronage.[24]

When an artisan from Gagliano told Cosimo that "never
have I wished for anything more in life than to take shelter

under the wing of your power and authority . . . while I live . . . so shall I always be completely faithful to you," he evoked an image strikingly similar to that of the popular devotional figure of the *Madonna della Misericordia*, under whose protective cloak the weak seek shelter (Figure 1.7). Patriarchal metaphors provided a means of associating the authority of fathers, patrons, and the Almighty. A kinsman and partisan of Cosimo de Medici addressing Averardo, Cosimo's cousin and chief lieutenant of the party, as "revered, as a father," declared: "You are my god on earth." Few friends of Cosimo's went so far as the friend who referred to Forese Sacchetti as his "Father, Son and Holy Ghost."[25]

The analogy between God the Father and Cosimo, Godfather to his friends, was spelled out in a letter from a former client, Branca Brancacci. In a virtuoso variation on the beatitudes and Christ's words in the garden of Gethsemane, Brancacci exhorted Cosimo to reverse the sentences imposed by the Medicean government upon its enemies: "Oh Lord have mercy upon us . . . blessed are the merciful, for they themselves shall have mercy . . . through your piety and singular grace, my father, I pray that this cup may pass from me: nevertheless, not my will but yours be done." There may well have been an element of irony in his prayer, as there surely was in Benedetto Dei's observation to his brother Miliano: "He who does not turn to the cross can not be saved, and thus I say, and have said, and will say, that he who does not turn to ally himself with the balls [a reference to the Medici coat of arms] will find his head and shoulders broken *(chi non*

1.7. *Madonna della Misericordia*, fifteenth-century wooden devotional statue.

*si volta a essere colle palle gli fie rotto la testa e lle spalle)."* But the active participation of most Florentines in religious confraternities, which were important places for meeting and making friends, enlivened these rhetorical forms with vital meaning.[26]

⁓

The concepts of charity and intercession and their role in achieving salvation, which relate instrumental friendships with earthly patrons to the protection and patronage of God and the saints, function as the essential link between personal patronage and the patronage of art that created the Florentine Renaissance.

Charity, the Christian face of patronage, involved not only aid to the poor and performing acts of mercy toward the general populace, but also promoting the community's spiritual welfare by building and decorating churches and chapels. This conception of charity, which patrons like Cosimo de' Medici hoped would balance the sinful weight of his bank's usurious gains at his own final accounting, was perfectly imaged in a fresco painted by Giotto in the Arena chapel for a Paduan merchant, Enrico Scrovegni. The fresco presents a visual model of the reciprocal relation between artistic patronage and salvation. This otherworldly transaction is represented in a scene of the *Last Judgment*. Scrovegni offers his chapel, supported by a friar, to the Virgin and a bevy of angels, who extend welcoming hands to him from heaven (Figure 1.8); by contrast, sinners below in hell are hanged by their money bags. These associations are similarly spelled out in Masaccio's radically original *Trinity* fresco in Santa Maria Novella, with its tour-de-force classicizing perspective, incorporating the donors in its unfolding of the central message of Christianity: the intercession of Christ with his heavenly Father to redeem the sins of corruptible mortals otherwise destined to molder in the tomb (see Figure 1.5).

An altarpiece painted in the late fourteenth century for the chapel of the confraternity dedicated to the *Trinity* in the cathedral was later re-sited on the east wall where it was prominent in the line of vision of worshippers exiting the church. The alterpiece has been described as a double intercession because it articulates the claims of the Virgin and Christ upon one another and represents their sacrifices as worthy of a reciprocal obligation on the part of God the Father to effect the salvation of their devotees (see Figure 1.6). The Virgin, chief intercessor for men facing the judgment of her son, Christ, and his heavenly Father, protects and presents the followers at her feet with her right hand; with her left, she indicates her breast, a gesture explicated by the inscription "Dearest son, because of the milk that I gave you, have mercy on them." In turn, the son displays the wound he suffered for the redemption of mankind while entreating, "My Father, let those be saved for whom you wished that I suffer the Passion." The dove of the Holy Spirit above him sweeps the viewer's eye upward along the line of the right hand of God to the aureole around his head, bright with the stars of heaven. The clear message of this image and

1.8. Giotto da Bondone, detail of *Last Judgement, Enrico Scrovegni Presenting His Chapel to the Virgin*, fresco, Arena Chapel, Padua.

its incorporated inscriptions is that man's access to God is through the intercession of Christ and the Virgin, just as earthly patrons intercede to procure their friends earthly protection and rewards.[27]

Representations of the friendship and patronage of the saints and the cult of the Virgin as chief intercessor for mankind accounted for an enormous proportion of Renaissance images in all media. The aim of the Renaissance artist to make visible the real world in a realistic setting facilitated the viewer's identification with these figures, as advocated by religious leaders like Archbishop Antoninus in his prescriptions for personal devotion. "When you have heard mass, or before, or if you want, in your own room, kneel before a crucifix, and . . . consider his face. First, the crown of thorns, ground into his head as far as the brain; then his eyes, full of tears and blood and sweat; then his nose, full of mucous and tears and blood; the mouth, full of bile and spittle and blood; his beard, similarly full of bile and blood and spittle, having been spat upon and raked; then his face, blackened and spat upon, and livid from the blows of the flail and the fist."[28]

Identification with the experience of Christ and other holy figures perceived as friends was further fostered by the sympathetic representations of the humanity of the saints in works like Fra Angelico's for San Marco. In the main altarpiece, the name-saint of Cosimo's recently deceased younger brother, Lorenzo, looks piteously out at the viewer from his place behind Cosimo. In the chapter room *Crucifixion*, Saint

Damian is humanized and individualized by his gesture that mourns the dead Christ, and perhaps his Medici devotee as well. The *Crucifixion* fresco in Cosimo's private cell (Figure 1.9), inserting his name-saint into the tableau at the foot of the cross with the inscription, "Son, behold your mother, Mother, behold your son," creates a personal connection between Saint Cosmas and the Virgin.[29]

Among the most human and personalized images of celestial friends and protectors are those of the archangel Raphael, protector of the young and travelers, exemplified by Tobias. A tale from the Apocrypha, set in Nineveh during the Jewish exile in Assyria in the eighth century B.C., tells of the journey of a young boy sent to Media by his blind father, renowned for his charitable acts, to collect money owed to him. Tobias is accompanied by his dog and a traveling companion, who is eventually revealed as the archangel Raphael. Under Raphael's protection, Tobias at length returns safely home, bearing an unguent made, at Raphael's advice, from the guts of a rare fish, which was able to ward off evil spirits and restore his father's eyesight.

A cycle of eighteen frescoes illustrating the Book of Tobit was painted around 1420 for the meeting place of the confraternity of the Bigallo, whose patron was Saint Tobias; its charitable practices included taking in abandoned children and burying the dead. In the second half of the century, interest in this theme increased dramatically. It was enacted in popular sacred plays and celebrated in poetic narratives such as those written by Piero de' Medici's wife, Lucrezia

1.9. Benozzo Gozzoli, *Crucifixion with the Virgin and Saints Cosmas, John and Peter Martyr,* fresco in Cosimo de' Medici's private cell in the convent of San Marco, Florence.

Tornabuoni, who at the beginning of her account of the *Life of Tobias* in *terza rima* called upon God to "send me Raphael as my guide and companion,/he whom you sent to accompany the only son of Tobias on unknown paths."[30]

Florentine painters made more of the surviving images of Raphael and Tobias from 1465 to 1485 than all other Italian artists combined. As Ernst Gombrich noted, some representations of this subject were primarily penitential, and probably commissioned by members of the two Florentine devotional confraternities dedicated to St. Raphael. Among such images were Neri di Bicci's *Tobias and three Archangels*, which emphasizes the heavenly trio, and Botticelli's *Trinity with Saint Mary Magdalen and Saint John the Baptist*, in which Tobias and his guardian are literally a footnote to the crucifixion.[31] Other paintings, like the Pollaiuolo brothers' panel now in Turin, or the London National Gallery painting from the workshop of Verrocchio (Figure 1.10), emphasize the human elements of the story: the angel's concern for his young friend, the dog that followed faithfully at their heels, and the remarkable fish. These are details in which David Brown has discerned the hand of Verrocchio's famous pupil, Leonardo da Vinci.[32] As Dante wrote in Canto IV of *Paradiso:* "The Holy Church appears to us with a human face in Gabriel and Michael, and the other [Raphael] who restored Tobit to health."[33] Such pictures were probably commissioned by Florentine fathers on the occasion of their young sons' departure on business to distant lands as visual prayers for their safe return, and perhaps also as affirmations of the compatibility of wealth with charity. In some pictures, the individualized features of Tobias suggest their votive function; among the more notable examples are the altarpiece for the Doni family chapel by Neri di Bicci's pupil and assistant, Francesco di Giovanni Botticini, which apparently includes a portrait of the patron's son Agnolo, and a panel by a follower of Baldovinetti with the inscription, "Raphael, health-giver, be with me forever, and as you were with Tobias, always be with me on my journey."[34]

Such ways of thinking and seeing, of relating heavenly and earthly patronage and friendship, shaped views of personal patronage in Florence even though this relation also involved the pursuit of profit and the violent and mutable passions of partisanship. This seems unimaginable to some historians, especially those who, in contemplating the past, are angered by evidence of inequality or injustice, often conceived inappropriately in terms of modern class conflict. Lauro Martines argues that subservience and resentment are the main themes of Renaissance poems addressed to patrons, which "tell us, in ideal terms, what patron-client relations were all about." He points to the use of courtly language borrowed from conventions of speech between servants and their lords and masters, or lovers and their ladies, expressing extravagant affection or extreme animosity, depending on whether the client or lover had been embraced or spurned.[35]

Most fifteenth-century Florentine poems imitated Petrarch

1.10. Andrea Verrocchio and workshop, including Leonardo da Vinci, *Tobias and the Angel.*

in employing the conventions and rhetoric of courtly love, and Renaissance men naturally elided the varieties of love (or hatred). But the poetry of love, or hate, was not a major vehicle for expressing perceptions of instrumental friendship as experienced by most fifteenth-century Florentines. These were revealed in images, as we have seen, but they were mainly articulated in private letters of recommendation between patrons and their friends. In these letters, relationships were constructed, defined, and negotiated through pleas for aid, promises of loyalty, and remonstrations when expectations were not met.

Many patronage letters spoke of the affection and love between friends. A man's interests might be recommended "because I am his friend and very kindly disposed to him," or "because he is a friend and relative of your and my own dearest friends."[36] Raffaello Bonciani wrote to Lorenzo de' Medici, Cosimo's grandson, that his request was prompted by "love and trust"; Piero de' Ricci, asking a favor of Cosimo's son Giovanni, assured him that "when something occurs to you that I could do that would please you, I will do it with love and fidelity" and signed his letter "your brother." Niccolò Bonvanni, also requesting Giovanni's help, appealed to the "affection" and "goodwill and love that Cosimo and all of you bear toward me and my family."[37]

Scholars tend to assume that such language does not reflect what they recognize as real feeling. And, indeed, as Paul McLean observes in *The Art of the Network*, patronage letters (like poems) were "a corpus of patterned discourse," fashioned in accordance with rhetorical and social conventions. It is often difficult to distinguish between the rhetoric of friendship and its real presence. Nevertheless, the language of friendship letters—extravagant to modern ears—should not be summarily dismissed as mere form. It needs to be construed in the context of other information about the relationship of writer and recipient, including the content of their letters.[38]

The majority of the hundreds of thousands of patronage letters from fifteenth-century Florence were addressed to members of the Medici family. Many were penned by men, particularly lower-class Florentines and foreigners, who did not have personal relationships with their Medici patrons.[39] Men of lesser status sometimes strove to flatter their superiors, and the courtly rhetoric of letters addressed to Cosimo from residents of other Italian cities reflected the realities of their own political and cultural experience. But whereas many patronage societies are characterized by a notable inequality between patrons and their clients, in republican Florence, it was only in the last decades of the fifteenth century that members of the large traditional ruling class ceased to regard themselves as equals of the Medici. Their earlier letters were couched less in courtly terms than in language derived from expressions of respect and reverence for kinsmen and the Lord, thus honoring the recipient while reminding him of ideal models for the relationship. Dozens of such letters from close Medici friends discussed in this book offer insights into the rich and complex texture of friendships within the framework of patronage.

The Medici family's most intimate associates often avoided customary greetings, signatures, and protestations in favor of simpler or more uncommon locutions, which seem to express personal feeling more successfully. Roberto Martelli signed off a letter to Giovanni: "Farewell my soul, and love me"; Ugo della Stufa replied to an invitation from Giovanni to join him at the Medici villa of Trebbio in the Mugello, "Would that it were possible to sprout wings to please you."[40] Affection, in addition to a self-interested desire to preserve the Medici party, is apparent in close friends' concern for the Medici family's health and welfare, particularly after they were exiled in 1433, and their distress at the deaths of Averardo, Cosimo's cousin and the Medici party's chief lieutenant, and his son, Giuliano, within a few months of their expulsion from Florence.[41]

Patronage was not primarily about personal feeling; its purpose was the pursuit of mutual honor and profit. The essential themes of patronage letters were the responsibilities, rights, and benefits inherent in the obligations of instrumental friendships. However, once these were established, they constituted a framework of trust within which personal feeling might safely flourish.

Friendships among members of patronage networks were nourished by the familial feelings that their language evoked. Obligations to love and fidelity were part of the patrimony of patrons and clients; sons inherited from their fathers the debt of love and affection owed to friends. Orlando de' Medici wrote to Piero di Cosimo in 1442, "recalling to memory the ancient friendship maintained between the men of our houses both past and present";[42] similarly, Cosimo de' Medici wrote to an unnamed recipient concerning the bearer and beneficiary of his letter of recommendation:

> Rienzo di Biagio is my dear friend, and similarly his father was always a friend of all of us here, and as he drew near to death, in his will he left in our hands the affairs of his son Rienzo, so that as you can see I am obliged in everything that concerns him to give him all my favor and aid. And since he will be coming here and will need your help and favor I have advised him that he should go to you, and that for love of me, in everything honest and reasonable you will give him your aid and favor, and thus I beg you that you should do so, considering whatever aid and favor you do for him as done for me myself.

This letter illustrates how patronage operated through a string, or chain, of obligations passed on from one generation, and one friend, to another. To the fifteenth-century ear, Cosimo's concluding phrases would have had the added resonance of Christ's memorable injunction to the faithful that "inasmuch as you have done it unto the least of my brethren, you have done it unto me."[43]

A familiarity conducive to the benevolence of the civic friendship envisaged by Aristotle was fostered by writing letters, visiting, and exchanging gifts, all fundamental obligations of patrons and their clients and friends. Ugo della Stufa apologized to Giovanni di Cosimo "for not having fulfilled my duty to write," while Iacopo Lottieri wrote from

Naples that it was so long since he had heard from Giovanni "that our old friendship seems to me extinguished."[44] The duty of the visit was equally compelling. Luigi Guicciardini lamented to Giovanni that "those of us who are persecuted by fortune can't often visit those whom we ought," but the prosperous Medici banker and friend Giovanni Tornabuoni was able to assure Cosimo in 1464 that while in the Veneto and Ancona, "I have made the obligatory visits to these cardinals and other friends."[45] Such visits refreshed relationships between friends while paying tribute to the patron's power.

Those who could not present themselves in person often sent gifts, which were certainly intended as tribute but also to give pleasure to their friends.[46] Zanobi Bonvanni wrote to the young Lorenzo in December 1465 from Vicopisano where he was the Florentine vicar, "Since I was too far away to be able to speak to you face to face, through faith, and with love, I consider myself to be with you in person . . . I've been hunting and bird-catching in these feast-days, wishing to do my duty." His note was accompanied by a gift of game (a pheasant and other birds), "although partridges are not to be had when the moonlight is clear."[47]

Gifts were also sent as consolation. Andrea della Stufa, hearing that his old friend Cosimo was seriously ill, went hunting and sent him five game birds and three pairs of partridge: "Perhaps next time we will have better luck . . . but for now, although this is not what you deserve, be patient, and may God preserve you in good health." At this time, the nuns of the convent of San Nicola made special sweetmeats for

Cosimo, dispatched with best wishes for his speedy recovery.[48] Once when Giovanni was prevented by illness from joining a hunting party in the country, a close friend sent him a brace of birds to compensate for his missing out on the pleasures their band of young friends were enjoying. In the same spirit, another friend sent him "a bundle of one hundred salted eels, which I beg you to eat with friends, and if the gift is not as much as you deserve, take our good heart in addition."[49]

Modern scholars are particularly cynical about the compatibility of friendship with patronage, even between social equals, when the obligation to mutual support overrode considerations of morality and justice, especially in the exercise of office. But in fact, such injustices may sometimes have been due as much to personal affection between friends as to the obligations of patronage. In 1445, when Ugolino Martelli, an intimate Medici family friend and near neighbor, was serving as Captain of Pistoia, he acceded to Piero di Cosimo's request to help a Medici client: "There is no way that I can say no to you concerning anything. However, I tell you that such people do not deserve to have you for their friend; I have warned him and let him know that if he becomes involved in any wrong-doing that I will punish him, believing that you will be happy about this if I do it for just reason."[50]

In Cicero's view, it was impossible to imagine true friends asking anything of one another that was contrary to good faith, honesty, or the good of the republic. Many of the

Medici requests fell into these categories, and some of those friends who saw themselves as the equals of their patrons protested against unjust recommendations. Not all of them followed the example of Agnolo Acciaiuoli who, as we shall see in Chapter 3, put an end to his friendship with the Medici partly on this account.[51]

But as Alberti's brutally pragmatic account of friendship acknowledged, no one could survive without friends. Scripture decreed that "he who is not with me is against me." Friends were needed as protection against enemies. Thus, Giovannni de' Lorini exhorted Piero de' Medici: "With the Psalmist I say to you . . . 'Deliver me from my enemies, for you are my refuge, etc.'" Giovanni Rucellai advised his sons that the best way to defend their fortunes was to avoid making enemies, since "one enemy can do more harm than four friends can do to help."[52]

Whether Alberti was really certain, as he wrote in response to a recommendation from Giovanni de' Medici on behalf of a client, that "if this were not a just request you would not ask it of me, nor make yourself his intermediary," we cannot know. We do know that he agreed to help: "Because I know this to be my obligation, I desire to do for you and your request whatever may result in the satisfaction of one who loves you," in respect of "the ancient benevolence between us *(la benivolentia nostra antiqua)*." In using this phrase, he may, as Luca Boschetto suggests, have been reminding Giovanni that true friendship involved virtue and honesty. Certainly, Alberti was asssuming, along with many other Florentines, that *benivolenza* was a natural part of instrumental friendship, generated in opportunities for association *(usanza)* such as letter writing, visiting, and gift giving. Just as the commissions of patrons of art were the essential frame within which an artist's creativity had to operate to solve problems of artistic expression, personal patronage was a necessary framework within which most Florentines had to seek affection, understanding, and shared pleasures.[53]

In the high-stakes friendships of statesmen in the Medici circle, the required rhetoric of carefully calibrated self-presentation could be hard to penetrate. The letters written at the turn of the fourteenth and fifteenth centuries by the Florentine notary Ser Lapo Mazzei to his friend Francesco Datini, a wealthy silk merchant of Prato, were by contrast astonishingly frank and relentlessly self-reflective. Concerned to capture all the nuances and ambiguities of their many-faceted relationship, Mazzei employed the entire spectrum of the fifteenth-century vocabulary of love and friendship, expressing a Renaissance understanding of that relationship, which differs in many ways from most modern views of it.

Ser Lapo was inclined to measure his friendship with Datini by the highest Ciceronian and Christian standards, and frequently found it wanting. "Francesco, my feelings for you are not those of Damon for Pythias, nor of Orestes for Pylades [the legendary friends of ancient Greek literature whose example Cicero invoked in his *De Amicitia*], who would die for each other, for friendship's sake . . . But neither am I one of the milk-and-water friends you meet nowadays; and may God keep you from adversity, for I would not be the first to flee."[54] If Mazzei and Datini were not invariably in "accord in all things, human and divine," as Cicero demanded of the truest friends, it seems that each found in the other, as Cicero had in Atticus, someone with whom anything could be discussed, and someone, as Cicero put it, "with whom I can make an unguarded joke or sigh familiarly."[55]

In September 1390, Datini approached Mazzei with a formal proffer of friendship, not uncommon in this society, which set their relationship firmly within the necessary social and public frame. The notary responded warmly that since "you want me for a friend, even though I bring you no profit, . . . by the trust *(fede)* that you demonstrate, which appears to me as a ray of love, I will strive and exert myself to make you happy . . . you may trust me as a son." Once he was formally defined as friend and honorary kinsman, Mazzei felt free "to delight" in discussing with Datini his innermost thoughts, "because we are two persons in a single soul," although he continued to sign his letters not with the informal "tuo," but as "vostro ser Lapo," as appropriate to the difference in their social status.[56]

The alchemy in this period by which formal contracts constituting relatives or friends could generate intense and instant intimacy may seem mysterious to the modern sensibility. Similarly, we might read as erotic, avowals such as Mazzei's declaration to Datini: "I am more enamored of you than you can imagine," or his confession, in a gush of emotion in the early years of their intimacy, to Francesco's wife, Margherita, that her husband had "bewitched him." In fact, Mazzei was using a language of courtly love that embraced a variety of admired objects. Christian love or *caritas* was also part of the Renaissance spectrum of friendship, and as the speakers at the *certame coronario* had agreed, God was man's only true friend. In his contribution to this event, Michele del Giogante had chosen to argue that *caritas* was not quite the same as *amicizia;* nevertheless, he conceded that "if by chance [the ties between friends] should weaken, charity reunites and binds them."[57]

Charity was indeed a common pursuit that united Mazzei and Datini and graced the secular aspects of their friendship. Mazzei was a devout Christian and served for twenty years as notary to Santa Maria Nuova, the chief charitable institution of the city of Florence. Although Mazzei worried that his unceasing attempts to bring his friend Francesco closer to God were not entirely successful, Datini's foundation of the charitable Hospital of the Ceppo in Prato in 1410 became a project very dear to his heart, with which he sought the notary's help and advice. Mazzei recommended appropriate objects of charity to the merchant, and drew up the final will in which Datini bequeathed most of his estate to the Ceppo just before his death. This institution memorialized its benefactor in a retrospective donor portrait by Fra Filippo Lippi, depicting him in the company of four of its officers kneeling before the Virgin (Figure 1.11).[58]

1.11. Fra Filippo Lippi, *The Madonna and Child Enthroned with St. Stephen, St. John the Baptist, Francesco di Marco Datini and Four Buonomini of the Hospital of the Ceppo of Prato.*

In this respect, at least, Mazzei's protestation that he could bring his new friend no profit was untrue. The notary was also instrumental in cultivating and managing a network of powerful allies to foster and protect the Florentine business and financial dealings of his friend from Prato. Acting as a mediator in such essential transactions as negotiating with the Florentine tax officials on his behalf, Mazzei helped to neutralize some of the enemies Datini made as an extraordinarily successful merchant.

Where Mazzei himself had taken up Datini's formal offer of friendship and immediately reframed their relations as those of father and son, he once chose to outmaneuver an astounded creditor of Datini's, whose court case against him threatened to upset the merchant's cherished charitable plans, by first persuading the creditor that he could not win his case and then sealing the deal by shaming him into forging an instant formal friendship with himself and Datini, which bound him to forgive the merchant's debts. Mazzei's account of the incident in a letter to Datini told how the man flushed (presumably with astonishment or rage), but then "succumbed to reason," meaning that he conformed to the pressure of social expectation, swearing to God before the altar of Santa Maria Nuova "to establish this friendship," which the notary considered as "a gift of God."[59] This episode illustrates the potential range and flexibility of the Renaissance idea of friendship and reflects also on the importance of forging trustworthy bonds with business associates.

However, Ser Lapo clearly felt conflicted about the element of patronage in his own relations with Datini. While he bowed to the necessity of playing by the rules of instrumental friendship to assist Datini's business and accepted the advantages of having a rich and influential friend as godfather to three of his ten children, one who arranged a favorable marriage for a daughter and found lucrative employment for a son, the notary strove to maintain their personal friendship as a relation of pure love between men of virtue. Mazzei once declared to his friend that "you have no servant or estate-manager more obedient," but hastily added that "not so much for you, as for God and my honor I do this," invoking Saint Paul's affirmation that love can "support all things."[60]

Ser Lapo's responses to the gifts and favors Francesco pressed upon him were unpredictable and often contradictory. Early in their friendship, he hastened to assure Datini that he was pleased to "use" his new friend in the accepted fashion, and occasionally he requested the merchant to procure him this or that commodity he craved, like the anchovies of which he was particularly fond. But ultimately, Ser Lapo feared to accept too much from Francesco, lest they become *amici mercadieri* or *amici pilucconi,* loving like merchants or beggars.[61] Whereas a convalescent Andrea Bartolini once sent cheerful word by a mutual friend to Giovanni de' Medici that his gift of a delicate dish of veal "has restored his good appetite to its pristine condition," when Datini sent Mazzei delicacies, like partridges, he protested, averring that he preferred plain food appropriate to a working man. On one occasion,

Datini's favors led the notary to reflect with shame on his own inappropriate behavior toward a friend: "I thought to sustain this friendship through external things rather than with inner spirit as I should."[62]

For all Mazzei's conflicted feelings through the years concerning Datini's attitudes and behavior toward him, their friendship was firmly founded on the many evenings the two men spent drinking together before the fire in one or other of their houses. As Mazzei once reminisced, "In tasting those good wines we did nothing but laugh." One letter that the notary wrote to his host upon returning to his own house after all that good wine is signed, "Your Lapo on Sunday night, very sleepy."[63] Without his friend, the merchant was often depressed; Margherita Datini wrote to Mazzei begging him to come and "tell Francesco some of your jokes, so that they may bring solace to his melancholy."[64] The notary's account of the merchant's death in a letter to a mutual friend showed how well he knew and loved his friend: "May God give him peace. Of his death I will tell you little, because it would take a whole quire: his suffering, and the speeches he made, and his passing, which was in our arms . . . For it seemed to him astonishing that he should have to die, and that all his prayers should be to avail."[65]

Cicero, Augustine, and other classical and Christian writers suggested that the genuine love between true friends was most clearly seen in their delight in one another's company, in the pain that attended a falling-out, in grief for friends lost to death, or in distress at a more temporary absence. There are many eloquent expressions of such feelings in the Florentine sources. Alberti observed that paintings, especially portraits, are precious because they preserve the lineaments of friends who have passed on. Dante captured the pain of parting in his description of "the hour in which the yearning/of seafaring folk returns, and melts their hearts/the day they have bidden sweet friends farewell."[66]

The friends of Cosimo de' Medici's younger son Giovanni often bemoaned his absence: "It seems to the *brigata* [our group of friends] a thousand years until your return." His nephew Lorenzo's childhood cronies, Sigismondo della Stufa and Braccio Martelli, were later to write to him in similar vein, as we shall see in Chapter 3. Alessandra Strozzi and Bartolomeo Cederni conveyed how much they missed the company of close friends on festive occasions with the quaint phrase "we called for you under the table." [67] A reflection on friendship in one of Leonardo da Vinci's notebooks is characteristically more oblique: "A man came to his friend whom he hadn't seen for a long time, and wasn't received by him as he felt he deserved to be. When he complained, his friend replied that (in his mind) he had never been separated from him."[68]

However, in view of all the uncertainties and ambiguities of Renaissance friendships, some men felt the need for a more formal expression or recognition of their bond, like the proffer of friendship with which Datini formalized his relation with Mazzei, as well as with several other friends. This constituted a contract in a society in which a public promise or handshake sealed marriage alliances and business deals. Other men felt the need of notarized documents and oaths sworn on the Bible, like the Sienese and the Florentine who in 1460, "on account of the great affection that bound them, swore on the gospels to aid and defend one another, to consider as a friend or an enemy whoever was so to the other, to love completely and delight in everything of one another's as if they had actually been two brothers." Having joined their right hands and exchanged a kiss, they put their signatures to this pact.[69]

Many Renaissance men sent their friends portrait medals of themselves as tokens of their affection. A Roman *quattrocento* medalist who called himself Lysippus, after the celebrated ancient Greek sculptor, made medals emphasizing the virtues of the recipients, recalling Cicero's observation in *De Amicitia* that "friendship cannot exist except among good men . . . for there is nothing more lovable than virtue." One sitter is identified on the obverse of a medal simply as "his friend Parthenius"; another is described as "a young man of excellent character," while on the reverse is inscribed within an oak wreath, "from Lysippus to his best friend." The most inspired of Lysippus' amicable conceits was a uniface medal with a smooth reverse, apparently intended to be polished as a mirror. The obverse bore a portrait of a young man, presumably the artist himself, with the inscription: "Admire on one side your own beautiful face; and on the other that of your servant," in accordance with the passage from Cicero's *De Amicitia:* "He who looks upon a true friend looks, as it were upon a sort of image of himself."[70]

By the early sixteenth century, the friendship portrait had become a sophisticated vehicle for the expression of friendship. *The Concert,* now attributed to Titian, is seen as representing, among other things, the sharing of mutual pleasures, of music as a unifier of men of all ages. Pontormo's double portrait of *Two Men with a Passage from Cicero's* On Friendship (Figure 1.12) has been identified with a work described by Vasari as a painting of two of the artist's closest friends, from a circle of artists, poets, and merchants who read Dante, Petrarch, and ancient texts together. One of the figures is holding a sheet of paper with a passage from Cicero's *De Amicitia:* "Friendship embraces innumerable ends; turn where you will it is ever at your side; no barrier shuts it out; it is never untimely and never in the way."[71]

The representation of friends and lovers in portraits was often related to the contest between poetry and painting as to which most effectively captured the real life of its subjects. This contest was rooted in a rivalry dating back to the ancient world. Mantegna's lost portrait of two friends—Janus Pannonius and Galeotto Marzio—was described in a poem of 1458 comparing the artist's skills to those of the most famous classical Greek painter: "As the hand of Apelles with its wondrous grace painted the Pellaean king [Alexander] with his faithful companion, so Galeotto breathes with Janus in one picture, a knot of unbroken friendship." Pannonius

1.12. Iacopo Pontormo, *Two Men with a Passage from Cicero's* On Friendship.

was a celebrated Hungarian humanist and poet, and his intimate friend and roommate at the school of Guarino da Verona in Ferrara, Galeotto Marzio, was a humanist and philosopher who faithfully accompanied Pannonius up to the very moment of his friend's death in flight from Hungary to Italy.[72] A friendship portrait attributed to Filippino Lippi of the artist and his patron, Piero del Pugliese, discussed more fully in Chapter 2 (see Figure 2.11), may in fact have been inspired by the Alessandro Braccesi poem that described it. But it, too, may be seen as part of a three-way conversation between poems, portraits, and friends in which the images act, like patrons and saints, as mediators or intercessors.[73]

The same might be said of the many pictures friends of the Medici commissioned to associate themselves with this powerful family. The most extreme example is Filippo Lippi's panel for the Alessandri depicting the Madonna and Child with donors and saints who are not their own onomastic protectors but rather those of the Medici, Cosmas and Damian, who appear as saintly "friends of friends." Antonio della Casa also requested permission from the works committee of the Medici church of San Lorenzo to commission an image of these patron saints of the leading family of the neighborhood, to be affixed to one of the columns opposite the pulpit.[74]

A number of Medici friends and supporters also commissioned representations of the Magi, perhaps because they too wanted to identify themselves in highly decorative images with these wealthy, wise, and pious men, but probably because this subject was almost a Medici icon. Botticelli's London *Adoration* tondo, which closely resembles the Angelico-Lippi tondo in the Medici palace in 1492 (Figure 1.13), can probably be identified with the one Vasari saw in the house of the Pucci, who were leading henchmen of the Medici party from the 1430s. An unusual variation on this theme may be seen in Botticelli's Uffizi *Adoration of the Magi*. This was commissioned by Guasparre dal Lama, an obscure and unremarkable man not closely connected to the Medici, who apparently hoped to establish some association with them through this painting of an iconic Medicean subject featuring recognizable portraits that have been identified as Cosimo and his grandsons, Lorenzo and Giuliano de' Medici.[75]

For their part, the Medici had Gozzoli incorporate into his Magi frescoes in the Medici palace chapel portraits not only of the immediate family but also of household familiars and most faithful friends. On the east wall (Figure 1.14) are Cosimo, his elder son, Piero, his younger son, Giovanni, his illegitimate son, Carlo, Piero's sons, Lorenzo and Giuliano, with Giangaleazzo Sforza and Sigismondo Malatesta, the young sons of Cosimo's closest foreign friends, and, at the rear, Giovanni Tornabuoni, a Medici relative by marriage. In a group on the west wall are portraits that have been identified as those of Neri Capponi, Luca Pitti, Nerone di Nigi Dietisalvi, Roberto Martelli, and Francesco Sassetti.[76]

1.13. Fra Angelico and Fra Filippo Lippi, *Adoration of the Magi,* originally in
the Medici palace.

1.14. Benozzo Gozzoli, *Procession of the Magi*, fresco, Medici palace chapel, east wall, including portraits of the Medici family and their friends.

Sassetti and Tornabuoni, managers of the Medici bank, in turn commissioned Ghirlandaio to paint fresco cycles, in which groups of their Medici friends were included, for the Tornabuoni family chapel in Santa Maria Novella and Sassetti's chapel in Santa Trinita (Figure 1.15). The depiction of Sassetti and his family alongside the Medici in the piazza outside the palace of government, in front of the loggia designed for the city's rulers, was certainly a visual claim to power by association from which Sassetti meant to profit. But these images, commissioned by a man who read Cicero's *De Amicitia,* represent a much richer conception of friendship, in which alliances with men blend with the honoring of God and the invocation of the friendship of the saints in assertions of the essential unity of the Florentine here with the hereafter.[77]

1.15. Domenico Ghirlandaio, *A Scene from the Life of St. Francis*, set in the Piazza della Signoria, incorporating portraits of the Sassetti and Medici families, fresco, Sassetti Chapel, Santa Trinita, Florence.

# TWO

# Where Did Friends Meet?

$\mathcal{D}$URING an outbreak of plague in 1484, the city's police magistracy issued a decree prohibiting Florentines from meeting. "No-one, of whatever status, rank or order he may be, should dare or presume to attend, gather or meet together in any company, either of the day or the night, of men or of boys, nor go to hear the singers on the benches where they usually perform, or go to any of the usual places where in other circumstances people are accustomed to gather together." The Studio—Florence's university—and all schools were to shut, and no one was to go to Wednesday morning market outside the church of San Lorenzo; nor should they stop to stare at "any charlatan or tooth-puller" or any other spectacle on the streets, presumably including the building construction sites where crowds of onlookers often obstructed traffic.[1]

This chapter explores the shared experience that fostered friendships among Florentines within the framework of civic life, particularly the goodwill *(benivolenza)* arising from propinquity and frequent association *(usanza)* Aristotle envisaged in his account of human society, created by households reaching out to neighbors, to connect individuals to a city held together by friendship.[2] Relationships were shaped and played out in the physical spaces of the city: the streets, street corners, outdoor benches and loggias, family palaces, churches and confraternal meeting places, workshops of artisans and artists, dinner tables and taverns, places of work, and the baptismal font.

Florence was what anthropologists call a "face-to-face society." Its population, about forty thousand for much of the fifteenth century, inhabited a compact area within the third circle of defensive walls, completed in the late thirteenth century (Figure 2.1). The city could be crossed on foot, east to west or north to south, in a little over half an hour. The wealthy lived in large palaces in the same districts as less well-to-do families, who might be crowded together in one or two rooms. Since an individual's security and advancement depended largely upon his personal relationships, the streets in which Florentines constantly crossed paths were important sites of the making and maintaining of friendships. This fact of Florentine life is underlined by Ghirlandaio's portraits of Francesco Sassetti and his family consorting with their Medici friends in a prominent public and civic space (see Figure 1.15).[3]

FLORENZA

2.1. View of Florence, called the "chain map," c. 1450.

Florentines were acutely conscious of social and political status, which derived from kinsmen and governed the selection of marriage partners and allies. However, the physical circumstances of the city also favored the development of personal relationships between men of various ranks and occupations who had interests in common. Such friendships were recognized and admired more by the classical Greeks than by the status conscious Romans; they were also fostered by the Christian commitment to universal love. As Augustine wrote in his *Confessions*, a work beloved by all those who followed Petrarch in adopting the early Christian father as their personal guide to self-knowledge, "there is no friendship unless You weld it between souls that cleave together through that charity which is shed in our hearts by the Holy Spirit." Later Christian teachings encouraged corporate solidarity, among fellow citizens, and within confraternal and conventual brotherhoods, rather than individual intimacies; but then most Florentines defined their identity primarily in terms of such collectivities as kin groups and neighborhoods.[4]

At the same time, Florentine attitudes to relationships between men of different social rank were distinctly ambivalent. In his poem on friendship for the *certame coronario*, the herald Anselmo Calderoni raised the question of whether friendship could really exist between rich and poor:

> The good, wise and shrewd Quintilian
> expounds for us another fine subject,
> how in haughty Rome

a poor man had a friendship with a rich one.
It happened that the rich man was taken by pirates,
and since his father didn't pay the ransom, they were
    enraged
and sold him to the butchers.
The poor man set out immediately to find him;
he died in his place and saved him from death.[5]

The plebeian Calderoni refrained from comment on the implications of this parable, but the rich ironies and frequent ambiguity of friendship between rich and poor are deftly sketched in the scene from the patrician Alberti's *On Friendship*, in which we are introduced to Buto, "A long-time domestic servant of our family."[6] Buto enters bearing a gift of rare and out-of-season fruits, the signs and tokens of a flourishing friendship. He is praised by the family as a true friend for his faithfulness and constancy *(fede e costanza)* and his goodwill *(benivolenza)*; these remain unchanged by alterations in the Alberti fortunes, as evidenced by his daily kindnesses.

While Alberti suggests that Buto may be morally superior to his masters, he is not regarded as an equal. He is admired for his acerbic wit—a product of privation—like many of the city's professional and popular entertainers with whom Alberti consorted. Most famous of these was the sardonic barber-poet Burchiello, who sent Alberti a poem declaring that Alberti's verses were dignified by the barber's use of them as a napkin: "Most fittingly my sweaty lips/I often wipe with your lofty poems."[7] Such men shamed the often empty rhetoric of the privileged and served as both a goad to their conscience and a reliable source of the merciless humor so much to the Florentine taste, as we will see from the trick Brunelleschi and his friends played upon the Fat Carpenter.

Through the character of Buto, Alberti also expresses his own reservations about friendship. Buto has become a great jokester because he is accustomed by perpetual poverty to live in the houses of those who will support him, "smiling and assenting." He soon begins to make fun of the Alberti family debate on *amicizia,* in which the learned protagonists cannot refrain from shouting, wrangling, and waving their hands and heads about, "saying many beautiful things about friendship, which when tested prove to be fables." He advises the discussants to be skeptical of the views of their kinsmen, who are "well-versed in eloquence, but concerning useless things. Believe me . . . nothing harms the ability to make oneself loved as much as being poor; become rich, and you will have more friends than you want."

This chapter examines, through the lives and writings of some particularly articulate citizens, the themes of commonality and difference, what was shared and what was not, by Florentine friends of various classes who associated closely with one another in the physical settings of the Renaissance city.[8]

Michele del Giogante, an accountant by profession, was a familiar figure in the streets of Florence. An author and anthologist of popular poetry, he was one of the singers, renowned for their feats of improvisation, who performed his repertoire on the benches outside the church of San Martino (Figure 2.2). Located in the heart of a major center of the city's wool-working industry, the piazza alongside the church was the main venue for popular entertainment. According to the singers, the audience who gathered in the piazza several times a week to be moved "to tears or admiration" by songs of love, war, or civic celebration, comprised both patricians and plebeians. The church was also the meeting place of the charitable confraternity of the Good Men (*Buonomini*) of San Martino, founded in 1422 by Cosimo de' Medici and Antoninus, archbishop of Florence, to aid the shamefaced poor. Wealthy benefactors came together with the mainly artisan officials, who identified and evaluated worthy beneficiaries of the weekly distributions of food and wine at the confraternity's door.[9]

In his tax returns, Michele identified himself and the house where he lived—in the Medici neighborhood of the administrative district (*gonfalone*) of the Golden Lion and the parish of San Lorenzo—with another outdoor meeting place, the Canto alla Macine (Figure 2.3). One of many corners in the city where the street widened to set off some large building, a palace or a church, forming a miniature piazza, the Canto alla Macine was named after an ancient mill situated there when the stream of the Mugnone still flowed in this area. Already in Bocaccio's time, it was a landmark on the route from the Porta San Gallo, the northernmost gate in the walls encircling the city, to the center of town. In the 1430s

2.2. Church of San Martino al Vescovo, venue for the performances of popular poets and for the charitable confraternity of the Buonomini of San Martino, mid-fifteenth-century sketch.

and 1440s, the immediate environs of the Canto alla Macine constituted a largely working-class neighborhood, which lay in the shadow of the huge new Medici palace rising on the adjacent block facing onto the Via Larga, now Via Cavour. The Canto was anchored by a group of shops, including a bakery, a butcher shop, and a tavern, patronized by the residents of many nearby houses.[10]

The Canto alla Macine was also associated with one of the city's many fantasy kingdoms that marked out its festive, ritual, and theatrical space. The plebeian company of the Armenians, called the Company of the Millstone, was connected to the nearby Armenian church. The Medici family and friends participated alongside the working men of the district in the company's theatrical performances. The Canto was also to be the rallying point for a group of "servers and lovers of the house of Medici" who, after the Pazzi conspiracy against them in 1478, wrote offering their services to "the magnificent and powerful Lorenzo, loved and desired as lord by we young men and boys of the canto della Macina, numbering thirty or more."[11]

Michele del Giogante was a prominent personality of this district. The large and socially disparate circle of his friends, including an unusually well-documented group of artisans, entertainers, and artists, knew him by the affectionate nicknames of *il forte* (the strong) or *del Giogante* (son of the giant); not even the tax officials who reviewed his returns called him by the names with which he was christened—Michele di Nofri di Mato. Michele was the author of a memory treatise on the model of those recommended by Quintilian and the author of *Ad Herennium,* then attributed to Cicero; he used one hundred places in his own house as cues to recall a range of subjects and symbols that constituted a veritable lexicon of Florentine popular culture. Like most entertainers, Michele had more than a smattering of knowledge of the classical texts and authors admired as authorities by Renaissance Florentines and sought to memorize them along with central events of the Christian story, characters from myth and legend, and famous figures on the contemporary civic scene that were the main threads with which his extemporizing performances at San Martino were woven.[12]

The first place Michele identified in his review of his house was the bench *(pancha)* outside it, "and I call it the first seat."[13] From the mid-fifteenth century, influential families attached monumental stone benches to the facades of their palaces. These benches, like those outside public buildings, were for the convenience of friends and associates who were waiting to see them on business—personal, familial, or political—or who were simply fulfilling their duty to make frequent visits and reaffirm their loyalty. However, already in the fourteenth century, benches of perishable materials, like wood or brick, are documented in account books and represented in street scenes from paintings and illuminated manuscripts, like the one from Virgil's *Aeneid* illustrated by Apollonio di Giovanni (Figure 2.4). As a singer at San Martino, Michele understood the role of benches in entertainment and sociability, and he may well have been one of those

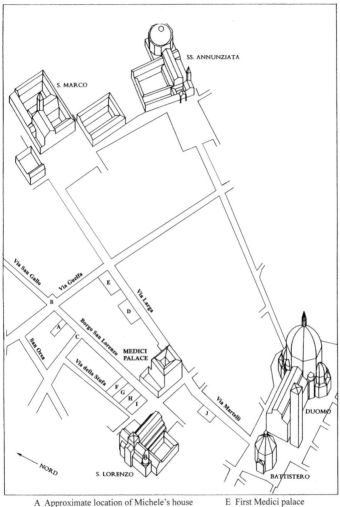

SS. ANNUNZIATA

S. MARCO

Via San Gallo

Via Guelfa

E

B

Via Larga

D

A

Borgo San Lorenzo

C

Santo Orso

MEDICI
PALACE

Via della Stufa

F G

H

I

J

Via Martelli

DUOMO

NORD

S. LORENZO

BATTISTERO

A Approximate location of Michele's house
B Canto alla Macine
C Canto del Bisogno
D Palace of Bernardetto de' Medici
  and Canto di Bernardetto

E First Medici palace
F Ginori palace
G, H Neroni palaces
I Della Stufa palace
J Martelli palace

2.3. Plan of the neighborhood of the Medici district of the Golden Lion and the parish of San Lorenzo.

2.4. Apollonio di Giovanni's illuminated manuscript of Virgil's *Aeneid*, fol. 87r, Riccardiana Library, Florence, showing in the center background a wood and brick bench.

who actually fulfilled Alberti's ideal, articulated in his treatise
*On Building*, of patricians and plebeians meeting on benches
"frequently and freely."[14]

As an eminent poet, performer, and anthologist of popular literature, Michele enjoyed the patronage of the Medici
family. But they were also friends by the Ciceronian measures
of constant association and common interests, "enjoying the
most complete agreement in policy, pursuits and opinions,"
particularly in shared cultural and charitable activities.[15] In
1450, when Piero de' Medici was nominated as one of a
group of ambassadors to be sent by the Florentine state to
acknowledge his friend Francesco Sforza's accession to the
lordship of Milan, he naturally turned to Michele. Michele
compiled for him at short notice a sort of briefing, a *quader-
nuccio* or notebook, which contained diplomatic and literary
accounts of Sforza's major military exploits. These were a favorite subject of the crowd at San Martino, since the *condottiere* was a great hero of the man in the street, or the *piazza*,
who enjoyed sallies like that of Antonio di Meglio in a frequently recited sonnet: "I then applied myself so well in
bed/that not even Sforza ever performed better in the saddle
than I."[16]

Michele invoked the pleasures of poetry and hospitality
they had shared when he asked Piero to help him promote
the career of a particularly talented young singer whom he
had befriended. "You already heard [him] sing in Lionardo
Bartolini's house, at a splendid dinner he gave for you, where
I brought him; he recited a few stanzas, you must remember

it. I think you were also acquainted with his work when he brought with him a very pleasing little book I made for him, and he had sung a good part of the material written in it at San Martino, including a little work Maestro Niccolò Cieco performed as a motet at San Martino, which made hundreds of people there weep in sympathy."[17]

Cosimo de' Medici arranged the marriage of Michele's only son, Piero, to Felicie, daughter of Antonio di Ugolino Martelli, who was assistant manager of the Venice branch of the Medici bank in the 1430s and 1440s and one of the family's closest friends. The Martelli were neighbors of both the Medici and Michele in the district of the Golden Lion and the parish of San Lorenzo. Michele's next-door neighbors and friends in the environs of the Canto alla Macine included Attaviano di Lupicino, trumpeter to the Signoria, and Ambrogio di Baldese, a painter associated with the workshop of the Gaddi brothers, famous for devotional pictures, whose account books Michele reviewed.[18] In view of the range of men with whom Michele associated in his neighborhood and in the practice of his professions, his many reflections on friendship throw much valuable light on its complex nature.

His poem on friendship written for the *certame coronario* of 1441 extolled the event and its organizers and briefly acknowledged the views of Homer, Virgil, and Cicero, as well as Dante and Petrarch. Scripture, however, was the source of Michele's conviction that "Of true friendship the witness/ was Jesus Christ; there is no other measure."[19] Nevertheless, the literary anthologies that he compiled with his friends

Sandro Lotteringhi and Giovan Matteo di Meglio, their hand-writing alternating in successive entries, include a broad selection of classical texts on love, affection, and friendship, a vernacular moral treatise on the evils of false friendship, and a large number of their own poems touching on these themes.[20] Other poems and letters Michele wrote show how hard he worked to cultivate human friendships, especially with his fellows in the entertainment business. He strove, as Cicero prescribed in *De Amicitia,* to be open and honest with his friends and to avoid even being suspicious and ever believing that his friend had done something wrong. If misunderstandings arose between them, he was eager to apologize and to effect a reconciliation.[21]

Michele became such close friends with Niccolò Cieco, a poet who moved to Florence from Arezzo in 1432, that he invited him in 1435 to live in his own house. An entry in one of Michele's anthologies describes how he had offended Niccolò; it is followed by the sonnet of apology he offered him. "Michele wished to take down in writing the stanzas [Niccolò] sang at San Martino in a correct manner, and with the aid of others, explained this to Niccolò, who replied that he was happy about this. Niccolò later became upset, and refused to sing any more. For this reason they didn't speak to one another for three days, after which Michele decided to make peace with him by sending him these three stanzas:

How much he who loves the truth is to be commended
and how much a friend should be valued . . .

how much a sincere soul should be commended . . .
and how much he should be trusted.
And therefore, knowing this,
and having a warm affection for you,
moved by a feeling of distress, not quite able to deal with
    this
unless I choose to take the blame entirely upon myself,
although without malice or evil design.
If any anger toward me should remain in your heart,
I beg you to grant me the pardon I ask."[22]

In March 1449, Michele addressed an apologetic sonnet to "Maestro Antonio who sings at San Martino." That day in the quarter across the river (Oltrarno), Antonio had run into Piero de' Ricci and told him that Michele had stirred up trouble and envy by comparing Antonio unfavorably to "that boy who sings at San Martino," possibly the young Simone di Grazia whom Michele had brought to dinner with Piero de Medici. After hearing this tale from Ricci, Michele was anxious to explain that he had meant no insult to Antonio that might "detract from the good friendship between him and me," and trusted that any wise man who might judge the matter would weigh that friendship appropriately in the balance.[23] Clearly, Florentine friendships among men of all classes involved issues of pride and honor, which being sensitive to social appearances, were as carefully calibrated by artisans as by patrician patrons and their political friends or clients.

Michele is often described as a client of the Medici; indeed, one literary scholar writing shortly after the *Risorgimento* called him their "gutless lackey."[24] But the relationship was much more complex than that, embracing both the strong attachment the poet clearly felt for all his friends and the pleasure he took in their common pastimes. Michele responded to the news of Cosimo's exile in 1433 with a passionate declaration of devotion in the language of a courtly lover: "I don't even know how I can begin/to set down either in prose or in verse what I want to say,/that I am yours in my very flesh and bones." Four years later, in the margin of a *zibaldone* in which he copied this poem, Michele noted alongside it that he had sent Cosimo a book of chess games, a gift celebrating a shared passion, since Michele had a chessboard hung above his bed, and Cosimo played with Magnolino, the chess champion of his day.[25]

Michele's poetry expressed the tension in his mind between the affection of friends and the servility implied in patronage. A sonnet addressed to Piero de' Medici's wife, Lucrezia Tornabuoni, at the behest of her husband and of Cosimo and his wife, Contessina, employs the conventions of a high-flown Petrarchan style, saluting her as: "Magnanimous, kind, discreet and gracious,/moving gently, benign, wise, honest and joyful . . ." But in another poem that he dedicated to Lucrezia, Michele reflected more critically upon their relationship, representing and addressing himself as a songbird unable to roam free, "showing the nature of your kind." Nevertheless, he told himself:

> If you look well at your golden cage,
> and then at the place where you dwell,
> appreciated as much as a great treasure,

> I think that had you the power to escape,
> short of being translated to that great choir
> by the wish of he who loves all souls,
> you would not hesitate an hour
> to return to those who value you:
> to the cage or the lap of your Lucrezia.[26]

A letter from Michele to Carlo di Palla Strozzi in Montpellier expresses much more directly than any he wrote to his Medici patrons several qualities that Cicero saw as characteristic of true friendship: a relaxed and affectionate intimacy, a warm concern for his friend's safety, and a desire to be with him again. But Michele was by no means the Medici family's "gutless lackey;" he reproached Cosimo quite sharply when the Martelli failed to produce the whole of his son's dowry, that "when I, not wishing to institute a new custom, wanted to know how much the dowry would be, before he took her home, you said to me, 'go on and take the girl and as to what remains to be paid, leave that to me.'"[27]

At the same time, as a Florentine patriot and a Christian, Michele deeply admired his powerful friend, loving him as much for his social as his personal self. In an extraordinary letter, Michele rebuked Cosimo's younger son, Giovanni, for failing to be at his father's side on Christmas day 1438:

> I am so astounded, and impelled by such astonishment and displeasure, that it is impossible for me to remain silent any longer, that you, having such a father for a head, of whom you are the limbs, and he being the most remarkable and ad-

mired man, not only now or ever of our city, but in the entire country, given that we are speaking of a private citizen and a glorious merchant and he to whom all the great affairs of Italy are entrusted, and furthermore he who preserves our city through his great acquaintance with all the spiritual and temporal powers, and with the help and support of his wisdom and his purse, and by that grace which our glorious God has instilled in him, of which the signs are his worthy deeds, to His glory.[28]

Similar questions about the quality of friendship between unequals arise when considering the relationships between the Medici family and the socially heterogeneous collection of all those who at one time or another resided within their great palace (Figure 2.5) or who were part of the daily ebb and flow of extended family, friends, and partisans in and out of the palace entrances and open loggias on the Via Larga, or from the piazza outside the church of San Lorenzo.[29]

These household familiars included doctors, artists, humanist tutors for sons, a resident priest to service the family chapel (Gentile Becchi at one time fulfilled both these latter functions), secretaries and factors who ran the Medici country estates, and for almost a decade, the Milanese ambassador, Nicodemo da Pontremoli, the envoy of Cosimo's closest foreign friend and ally, Duke Francesco Sforza. In the 1430s, after their father's premature death, Cosimo had taken into his previous house on the Via Larga the three young sons of

Giovanni Portinari, manager of the Venice branch of the Medici bank. Letters between the thirteen-year-olds, Pigello Portinari and Giovanni de' Medici, testify to their close friendship and the experiences they shared, including their efforts to master the abacus. All three Portinari boys went on to assume positions of trust in the Medici banking organization, Pigello as manager of the important Milan branch. Of course, the relations of the Medici family with those who worked for them within the palace were framed by patronage; but the traditional extension of family to incorporate neighbors and friends was naturally animated, as the Aristotelian view of civic society envisaged, by familiarity and goodwill (*usanza* and *benivolenza*) arising from common interests and dedication to common enterprises.[30]

One of the most interesting of the Medici *familiari* was Ser Alesso Pelli, a notary whose professional duties as the ratifier of social contracts, from marriages and business agreements and property transactions to wills and records of birth, made him a man to trust and a mediator among various social groups and strata. Described by the chronicler of the convent of San Marco as "much frequenting" Cosimo's house, Ser Alesso was indeed a factotum of the Medici household in the late 1430s and early 1440s, when the family still lived in the "old house" (*casa vecchia*), as it became known after they moved into the new palace in 1459. Many of Cosimo's letters from this period, and almost all those of his wife, Contessina, were written in Alesso's hand. Alesso's own letters illuminate the relationships of the Medici house-

2.5. Medici Palace, Florence.

hold and those who frequented it, to dine or to visit, on political, banking, or personal business.[31]

The major purpose and theme of Alesso's letters was the gathering and sharing of information—in the palace and at church, in the *piazza* and on the streets, in the city or at the Medici country villas or the curative baths—for the promotion of common Medicean interests and goals. By no means were all of these political, although Alesso's letters overflowed with details of elections and diplomatic missions and battles, and at the Medici dining table, he would pass on to Cosimo what he had learned in the piazza about public opinion concerning these events.

Alesso was a faithful servant of the Medici household and its interests. But he was no Buto. Undoubtedly, he owed some of his influence in charitable, pious, and cultural circles to the patronage of the Medici, but he was as dedicated to these activities as they were, and well-fitted for them by education and native ability. Much of Alesso's notarial business was done in the Medici neighborhood for their family and friends. In 1441, he was one of two witnesses of the document recording the gift of Niccolò Niccoli's humanist library by his trustees, among them Cosimo and Lorenzo de' Medici, to the convent of San Marco, which Cosimo de' Medici was then rebuilding. Together with Messer Mariano Salvini, general of the Servite Order, Alesso supervised the boys' religious brotherhood of the Purification, which met at San Marco. He also served as one of the twelve *Buonomini*, the charitable confraternity Cosimo founded to aid the shamed poor at the church of San Martino, where Michele del Giogante and his friends performed their popular poetry. Francesco Inghirami, manager of the Florentine branch of the Medici bank after 1454, wrote to Cosimo's elder son, Piero, with the news of Alesso's death in 1461: "Ser Alesso has passed away, which has upset his whole band of friends *(tuta la brighata)*, but especially the poor."[32]

Alesso was an affectionate friend and advisor to Cosimo's sons, and he took obvious pleasure in their company. He observed that in writing to them, he wanted "to abandon pedantry and the notary's style, and not to be so serious." In 1439, he confessed to the eighteen-year-old Giovanni, then staying in the Medici castle at Trebbio in the Mugello: "I envy you this trip in weather as fine as I have ever seen. I'm sorry now that I didn't come with you." Another time he told Giovanni how much he regretted that he couldn't join him in Prato for a fair, because "I needed to be with you to see the noteworthy things that happened to you; remember them so you can let me know when we see each other."[33] When the nineteen-year-old Giovanni was again visiting Trebbio with his brother, Piero, Alesso begged them to "economise so that you don't spend too extravagantly, and also don't get over-heated and don't become depraved with those good-for-nothings . . . I am so worried about all these things that I'd like to be there to take care of them." He was clearly fond of Mona Contessina, Cosimo's wife, and once teased her that if she didn't reply more promptly to his letters, he would keep her on leaner rations in future. On another occasion, in a note announcing that he and the men of the household would be arriving that evening at Careggi, he begged her to have something really nice for them to eat: "chestnut cake *(castagnaccio)*, not pork rinds *(cotenuzze)*"; his father had owned a small wood of chestnut trees, so perhaps *castagnaccio* had been a childhood treat.[34]

Alesso joined in the fun when the Medici participated in the festivities of the working class confraternity that met in the Armenian church near the Canto alla Macine; a letter to Cosimo from his younger brother, Lorenzo, who died in 1441, asked him to get Ser Alesso to "dig up a cloak in the Greek style." Alesso was an habitué of the *canto*, and young Giovanni de' Medici was enjoined in one letter from a mutual friend that if he failed to pass on Alesso's greetings to all his friends who frequented it, the notary would not dare to show his face there again. Several of Alesso's letters refer to the Medici family's annual celebrations of the feast of Saints Cosmas and Damian, which he helped to organize; one letter from Trebbio from 1442 paints a vivid picture of the household at play together. "Cosimo is very well indeed and we are passing the time very happily occupying ourselves with pruning the trees in the park, and we are looking forward to the festival like children . . . I can't say more as they are calling me to come and clean up and burn off."[35]

When in the mid-1440s Giovanni made a trip to Aquila without asking Cosimo's permission, Alesso wrote to warn him that "your trip has caused great anguish, especially to Mona Contessina; Cosimo makes light of it." In succeeding days, Alesso continued to report the family's reaction to Giovanni's misstep: it had "upset Cosimo more than he wants you to know . . . since he didn't expect to see the day when you would return to alleviate all this anxiety . . . I have never seen him so grieved as when he heard you had gone . . . when you get back you will have trouble going as far as Careggi [the Medici villa on the outskirts of Florence]."[36]

It was Alesso, regarded as something of an expert on building *(nel murare et nello hedificare)*, who wrote to Giovanni in 1445 describing the clearing of the site for the new Medici palace: "You wouldn't believe the size of it . . . and the destruction of the *canto*, from Zanobi's house to Fruosino's, and everything has been torn down, which is a magnificent thing to see." Later he advised Giovanni on the problems of procuring water for the villa he was building on a steep hill in the environs of Fiesole: "I wasn't able to discuss with you yesterday what I wanted to, because I had so many other problems. I'll just tell you by this note that that construction in the piazza is not the way to get water; the way to get water is this: to make a channel across the piazza . . . and because I can't explain all this at length by letter I need to come [and show you]."[37]

Twenty years later, it was Giovanni's turn to advise Alesso, an old man still sticking to the classical and Christian rules of duty and resignation to fate that he had learned in the schoolroom. In 1457, Giovanni had invited Alesso to join him; the notary replied that he was so ill that "I don't see how I can come, either for my sake or yours . . . so go with

God and pity me, for I can't go on." Nevertheless, in May 1461, we find him writing to Giovanni again, from Pisa, where he was serving as one of the officials entrusted with constructing a canal to keep its port from silting up. This endeavor was so crucial to Florentine commerce that Lorenzo de' Medici himself was twice to assume that trying office. Alesso described the terrible conditions in which they were working: "infinite effort, discomfort and exertion, unusually great heat without respite in the open air, on land and on sea exposed every day to the sun."[38]

However, Alesso refused to accept his recall to Florence, apparently at the instigation of his powerful friends concerned for his welfare. As he explained to Giovanni:

> I received your letter . . . and understand [that you think] it is regrettable that I should stay here, and that I should return. Omitting the requisite thanks, I shall come straight to the point. After much persuasion by the Officials of the Canal I came to this job, not in any hope of gain, for there is no compensation for the danger to my life, since eight of the principal workers on this site have died . . . but I cannot so easily leave without great damage to the operation . . . everything I have done is for the great benefit to the commune that I see flowing from it . . . I will remain here while I live.[39]

Like the ideal friend described in Cicero's *De Amicitia*, Alesso had lived under the same roof as Cosimo, sharing public and private cares and a conviction that each was indispensable to the service of his city. In the course of his life,

Alesso had often profited from Medici patronage, but at the end, he refused their aid to preserve his honor. He asked Giovanni in his last surviving letter "to excuse me and to explain to our friends and others as you think best . . . Don't write to Cosimo . . . because I have written so much to him that I think I have bothered him too much . . . I will let our band of friends *(brigata)* know when I leave . . . I think I may [return] soon, for San Giovanni." Whether he made it home on June 24 for the festival of Florence's patron saint, John the Baptist, we do not know. He died four months later.[40]

Ser Lapo Mazzei, Ser Alesso Pelli, and Michele del Giogante were highly literate men who left unusually full accounts of their reflections on the friendships they made in the course of daily life: around the neighborhood, at work, in churches and confraternities, and at dinners and public performances of poetry and sacred plays. The record of most men's experience, in an era in which self-examination was largely restricted to the confessional, is more fragmentary. We may assume that some shared the apprehensions of Giovanni Morelli or Messer Paolo da Certaldo concerning the dangers they discerned in the city's intense social life, but Giovanni Rucellai could tell his sons that he had enjoyed the "favor and goodwill *(gratia et benivolentia)* of his kinsmen and relatives and neighbors and all the rest of the men of the *gonfalone.*"[41] At the same time, a variety of sources suggest that the love and friendship generated by propinquity and frequent association on the urban scene could be a complex and often ambiguous experience.

The many activities centered on local churches offered myriad opportunities for the formation of friendships among parishioners and other near neighbors. These are particularly well documented for the church of Santa Maria del Carmine in Oltrarno, in the parish of San Frediano and the district (*gonfalone*) of the Green Dragon. This was a largely working-class area with a particularly high proportion of artists and craftsmen among its residents. Parishioners gathered at the church not only for services, and as devotees of the cult of the miraculous Madonna del Popolo housed there, but also to dispense charity to the neighborhood poor and to partici-pate in the activities of the confraternity of Sant'Agnese, re-corded by Neri di Bicci, the painter who served for many years as its syndic. The artist Fra Filippo Lippi also began his career in the Carmelite convent, for which he performed a va-riety of small services.[42]

The highlight of Sant'Agnese's activities was the perfor-mance of the sacred play of the Ascension. Its scenery and astonishing technical effects drew spellbound crowds from all over the city and beyond. Also located in the church of the Carmine was the Brancacci family chapel, in which Masaccio and Masolino began in the 1420s to paint their revolutionary fresco cycle of the Life of Saint Peter, eventually completed by Filippino Lippi half a century later. In accordance with Saint Augstine's sense of "the present time of past things," the neighborhood community is vividly portrayed in these paintings depicting the miracles of the saints, as enacted in the piazza right outside the door of the church (Figure 2.6).[43]

The pious lay confraternities that met in churches were the focus of an especially intense form of sociability. Although few membership rolls have survived, it is estimated that a very high proportion of Florentine men belonged to confraternities, of which there were about 150 in the city in the fifteenth century. There is ample evidence in poems, prayers, and sermons written by members of these associations of the intense religious feelings that united them in devotion. The charitable obligations of confraternal communities also drew them together in the biblical command to "love thy neighbor as thyself," although few confraternities went as far as the penitential company of the Archangel Raphael, which expressed in its statutes, the desire "that this love of God and neighbor be understood not only as extending to our friends, that is, to the brothers of this company, but also as extending to enemies and strangers."[44]

Religious fervor in this period often had a sexual tinge; a nun's designation as the bride of Christ was taken literally, and a seventeenth-century lesbian nun confessed to nightly ecstatic communion with a fellow sister, in the guise of a beautiful angel called "Splenditello."[45] In the paraliturgical activities of confraternities, feeling had freer reign than it did in church. Singing hymns, self-flagellation, delivering impassioned sermons, and enacting stirring sacred plays facilitated the blurring of boundaries between the varieties of love— fraternal, charitable, spiritual, and erotic. Particularly popular

2.6. Masolino, Brancacci Chapel, Santa Maria del Carmine, Florence, *Saint Peter Healing the Lame Man and the Raising of Tabitha.*

in this period was a prayer by Iacopone da Todi that urged worldly friends, "moved by holy madness," and "every lover who loves the Lord," to "join the dance singing of love,/ come dancing all impassioned."[46]

Even within the mainstream of devotion and charity, the love of some confraternal brothers might verge on wilder shores. In his *Book of Dreams* of 1568, Gian Paolo Lomazzo made Leonardo da Vinci, whose homosexual inclinations were well known, the spokesman for his view that "the love of men *(l'amore masculino)*" is solely a work of virtue, and joins males together in various sorts of friendship, so that out of these at a tender age come, at a manly age, worthier and closer friends."[47] Whereas Ser Lapo Mazzei had used the language of sexual love to express a chaste friendship for Francesco Datini engendered by *caritas,* in 1476, an informer denounced the carpenter Piero di Bartolomeo to the Officials of the Night for sodomizing Bartolomeo di Iacopo, son of a grocer, behind Piero's workshop near the Old Market but explained that Piero acted "out of great love and good brotherhood because they are in a confraternity together, and he did as good neighbors do."[48]

Besides dispensing charity, the major functions of pious confraternities were to perform penitence or to sing the praises of the Lord. The festive companies like that of the Armenians at the Canto alla Macine often distributed charity, but they were also playful, dividing the city into imaginary kingdoms that held rival processions on feast days, especially that of the city's patron. Later in the fifteenth century,

*compagnie di stendardo*, or *compagnie di piacere*, brotherhoods dedicated to diversion under the flag of pleasure, were founded
in the carnival spirit of inverting established values. They
parodied devotional confraternities, as we may see from the
subversive statutes Machiavelli drew up for one such band
and by the name of another, "Three Nails of Christ, who
meet at the canto de' Ricci," an irreverent reference to the
instruments of the Passion, the nails that pierced Christ's
hands and feet upon the cross.[49]

Rather than loving one another, the brothers of these
companies were encouraged to envy. Although they often met
in churches, their main activities were dining and gossiping,
not devotion. They did not take vows of silence or solitude;
instead, they were punished for being silent or for failing to
go to "all the lunches, teas, dinners, comedies, and parties"
that they could. The coppersmith Bartolomeo Masi, who
had once been a member of the boy's devotional confraternity of Saint John the Evangelist, later joined no less than
five *compagnie di stendardo* and founded another himself, which
was dedicated primarily to dining.[50]

Dining together was an acknowledged sign of friendship,
although precisely what this custom reveals about that relationship varies widely according to the social context, the
participants, and the venue. For example, the wary merchant
Morelli issued dinner invitations to his home more as a
means to mollify envious neighbors who might otherwise become enemies than as an expression of a desire to commune
with friends. Paolo di Messer Pace da Certaldo warned against

drunkenness that lowered a man's guard and might lead to his revealing too much of himself.[51] It is not clear whether the dinners of the brotherhoods dedicated to pleasure were in private houses or in taverns; pious confraternities forbade their members to frequent the latter because "God does not dwell there," just as they proscribed the associated vices of sodomy, playing dice or cards, and blasphemy.[52] The Osteria del Fico (the inn of the fig tree) proved the undoing of such notorious antisocials as Antonio Rinaldeschi, who in a drunken rage after losing at gambling, flung dung at a street-corner image of the Virgin and was hanged for blasphemy (Figure 2.7).[53]

The antiauthoritarian parish priest Arlotto, whose nickname means "slovenly glutton" and who assembled an irreverent collection of amusing *Motti e Facezie* (jokes and sayings) recounting the repartee he exchanged with many famous figures on the Florentine scene with whom he was invited to dine, met his friends at least three times a week at his favorite tavern, where he kept a running tab. This was the Albergo dell'Uccellatoio (the inn of the bird hunters) on the Via Bolognese, some nine kilometers north of the Porta San Gallo; the building, even if much altered, still survives. For Arlotto, the tavern was a place to enjoy himself conversing with his many friends (including the Archbishop of Florence, who took these occasions to deliver homilies against drinking too much), as well as an opportunity to winkle a free meal out of his wealthier acquaintance.[54]

When Arlotto's close friend Bartolomeo Sassetti, the merchant and Medici friend who kept their accounts for the construction of the Medici palace and the church of San Lorenzo, suggested that perhaps Arlotto should go to the Uccellatoio less often, the priest replied: "I accept your reproof, coming from a dear friend, as I know you have always been to me, and I understand that you are doing your duty as a friend." He added that Archbishop Antoninus, "who loved me heartily and with whom I was on very close terms," had made the same suggestion, to which he had responded that as a great lover of company, he had once kept open house for his friends. But this left him little time to read his breviary and severely depleted his meager resources. Now, "they take me to the tavern out of friendship, and I go there out of charity, and usually they pay for me."[55]

More conventional men of means preferred to honor their friends and neighbors, as Morelli advised, by inviting them home to dinner, thereby literally demonstrating the extension of the family to include chosen companions outside the domestic circle. Citizens serving on the Signoria were sequestered away from family and friends in the palace of the Priors. Although in view of the number of ceremonial meals served to honor diplomatic visitors, they dined rather well there, one man invited his colleagues home on the very night their term of office ended as a sign that they had become his friends: "The last night, after we left the Palace, I gave a dinner for everyone at home *(alla dimesticha)* because we served in that office together in great accord and love."[56]

Vespasiano da Bisticci, the stationer and bookseller who

2.7. Filippo Dolciati, *Antonio Rinaldeschi at the Osteria del Fico,
Losing at Gambling.*

provided books for the libraries of Cosimo de' Medici and of the convents of San Marco and the Badia, which the Medici furnished, was famous for his appreciation of the pleasures of the table. He liked to share these, and the beauty of his home, with friends such as Bartolomeo Cederni, who lived quite close to Vespasiano's bookshop in the city. One particularly beautiful spring, in mid-May 1471, the bookseller repeatedly pressed his friend to come to visit him at his country villa at Antella: "Do hurry up and come down here . . . because the flowers, the trees and the woods await you, and the birds are singing . . . come and enjoy this verdure, for we can have no greater pleasure than this."[57]

Vespasiano also shared with his circle of friends and customers his love of books and learning, which was the basis of his friendship with many of Florence's most powerful citizens. Among them were Cosimo de' Medici and Palla Strozzi, Cosimo's greatest Florentine rival in wealth, intelligence, and influence, whose library was even more distinguished than Cosimo's, and who was exiled in 1434 more on account of these compelling attributes than for any political opposition to the Medici.[58] Once when Vespasiano professed embarrassment, in view of his inferior education, about writing to Giannozzo Manetti, the noted humanist responded describing their friendship in explicitly Ciceronian terms: "Although I understand that this is a gracious rhetorical gesture, even if it were as you say, you know very well that we are friends, and true friendship, such as I believe we enjoy, can only exist between equals. So that insofar as by chance I might happen to have greater status than you in matters of erudition and learning, nonetheless our friendship "encompasses everything between us."[59]

Of course the offering of hospitality was not always the sign or start of a faithful friendship. Many classical, courtly, and Renaissance tales tell of betrayal, murder, or violence at dinners and banquets. Boccaccio's *Decameron* recounts the story of Nastagio degli Onesti, a young man renowned for his frequent invitations to friends to lunch and dine with him. Nastagio frightened his reluctant ladylove into marriage by inviting her to a banquet where she witnessed the miraculous reenactment of a knight hunting down his lady and having her devoured by two dogs for her cruelty to him. This macabre moral legend was the somewhat bizarre choice of subject for four wooden decorative panels by Botticelli, thought to have been made in the 1480s for the nuptials of a member of the Pucci family. The prominence of the Medici arms in the central scene of the banquet (Figure 2.8) likely serves to acknowledge or advertise Lorenzo's role as broker of the marriage, a pictorial record such as we have seen before of the close ties of friendship, here forged by a Medici patron's intercession or mediation on behalf of his friends.[60]

A colorful example of the real-life betrayal of the camaraderie of the board also relates to the Medici and their friends. Piero de' Medici, along with his friend Michele del Giogante, had enjoyed the hospitality of Lionardo Bartolini's house in the 1450s, when hosts and guests took shared pleasure in the performance at dinner of talented popular poets

2.8. Sandro Botticelli, *The Wedding Banquet of Nastagio degli Onesti*, panel illustrating a tale from Giovanni Boccaccio's *Decameron*, depicting a banquet typical of Lorenzo de' Medici's Florence.

and singers. No doubt those present admired the Bartolini family's three great panels painted by Paolo Uccello depicting *The Battle of San Romano*, with men and armor and horses represented in tour-de-force perspective. Apparently, Piero's elder son, Lorenzo, was among those who saw them on visits to his family's old friends and allies; in 1480, after they refused his request to pass the panels on to him, Lorenzo sent a crew of henchmen, including the renowned woodworker Francione, to the Bartolini palace at dead of night to carry them off to his own palace.[61]

It seems that Giovanni Morelli was correct in his suspicion that the hospitality necessary to cultivate friends could lead to a dangerous envy of a man's possessions. Attendance at formal dinners might also expose underlying social tensions in even the closest of quotidian friendships. The notary Ser Lapo Mazzei and the wealthy merchant Francesco Datini often laughed happily together over a glass of wine in front of a fire burning in one or other of their hearths, but Mazzei begged his rich friend "not to drive me away with great banquets," preferring to be visited or invited to dine "not in the manner of the court of Avignon, but in that of true Florentine friends, if such there be."[62]

A particularly interesting glimpse into the texture of friendship and the behavior of friends is offered by one of the most popular comic tales of the fifteenth century concerning the trick played upon "*il grasso legnaiuolo* (the Fat Carpenter)," one of a band of close friends who were in the habit of dining together. Grasso might well have felt that dinners with friends were more dangerous than pleasurable after he became the butt of the group's elaborate practical joke engineered by the architect Brunelleschi. The tale, told by Brunelleschi's biographer Antonio Manetti, turns on the friends' familiarity with the details of one another's daily habits and on their readiness to cooperate in making a fool of one of their number. It appears to be substantially true. Manetto Amannatini, nicknamed "the Fat Carpenter," is documented in the historical record, along with many of the twenty-two coconspirators, most of them artists or their patrons, who were bent on convincing Manetto that he had become someone called Matteo and was no longer himself.

The action is explained partly as the expression of Brunelleschi's natural ingenuity, and partly in terms of status, honor, and shame, important even among social intimates. Speculating on why Grasso refused to join them at dinner one evening, his friends, unable to find any reason other than a whim, and feeling themselves slightly ridiculed, "since they were almost all of a higher rank and status than he, amused themselves by imagining how they might take revenge for this insult." Grasso, after allowing himself to be duped, in turn felt that he had lost face with all his friends and left Florence. He went to Hungary, where he became a rich man, thanks to the patronage of Filippo Scolari, the Florentine *condottiere* known as Pippo Spano, who was captain of the King of Hungary's army. Encountering Brunelleschi again upon his return home many years later, Grasso, far from showing himself outraged or offended, embraced the architect as the author of his good fortune and his dearest friend.[63]

The plot to deceive the Fat Carpenter was set in motion when Brunelleschi visited him in his workshop "as he had a thousand times before." Prominent in the circle of Brunelleschi's friends and dining companions, "members of the governing group and masters of various creative crafts, such as painters, goldsmiths, sculptors and wood-workers" who used to get together to talk about their work, and who cooperated in Grasso's deception, or later recounted the story, were his fellow artists Donatello, Michelozzo, Rossellino, Buggiano, Scheggia, Luca della Robbia, and the poet and writer Feo Belcari. Some of the most interesting and best-documented Florentine friendships were those between artists who formed companies with one another, or worked side by side on the century's great public commissions, such as the decoration of the cathedral and the church of San Lorenzo.[64]

Artists' workshops often cooperated in the various phases of production of objects like altarpieces and devotional images. For example, the painter Neri di Bicci colored and gilded a number of gesso and marble figures made by the sculptor Desiderio da Settignano. Artists' fantastical nicknames for one another—Michelangelo's workshop alone contained dozens of characters, among them the radish, the stick, the oddball, the gloomy, the little fibber—express bonds of affectionate, if somewhat acerbic, familiarity between these fellow workers, similar to those that linked Brunelleschi, Il Grasso, and their circle.[65]

For artists, as for many other artisans, the hundreds of workshops that dotted the inner city were the center of their social as well as their working lives. Crucial to the deception of "the Fat Carpenter" was the rearranging of his workshop, the benchmark of his identity. Often open to the street, and to the gaze of passersby (Figure 2.9), artists' workshops were natural meeting places, and not just for sexual encounters between men and boys, although some 15 percent of those rendezvous reported to the Officials of the Night took place in workshops.[66]

Workshops and works committees of the city and its guilds and churches, responsible for building and decoration, were also natural sites of cross-class sociability, meeting places where artists and their patrons cooperated in the creation of works of art and became friends in the process, united by their common interest in considering how best to produce a work that might bring honor and fame to them both. The Fat Carpenter became convinced that he was mistaken about who he was when "Giovanni Rucellai didn't recognize me, he who's always in my shop." Rucellai was described as being "very well known to Grasso, who at this time was carving the top of a frame for a Madonna for him."[67] Similarly, Francesco Bongianni "often went to the workshop" of Lorenzo di Credi, who in the mid-1490s was working on an altarpiece that included a portrait of the patron as a donor; there, Bongianni also caught up on the latest gossip about Savonarola, the radical religious leader who dominated Florentine politics in this period.[68]

While these conversations between patrons and artists are lost to us, comparisons of contracts, preparatory drawings, and the finished works of art provide clues as to how their

2.9. Stradano, *Scene of the Old Market*, c. 1561, fresco, Sala del Gualdrada, Palazzo della Signoria, Florence. The Old Market was the commercial center of the city, where many shops were located.

ideas were altered and refined in continuing exchange as the work of art developed. Notable changes were made to Ghirlandaio's 1485 commission to fresco the Tornabuoni family chapel in Santa Maria Novella. These were related to religious and devotional concerns as well as to the commemoration of the family, as the number of portraits was increased, and the painter worked through alternative solutions to compositional requirements.[69]

Letters document this process when patron and artist were separated by circumstances. Piero de' Medici was absent at his country villa over the summer when Benozzo Gozzoli was finishing the frescoes for the chapel of the Medici palace, but the artist communicated frequently with his patron, with the help and mediation of the Medici friend and bank administrator Roberto Martelli. On one occasion, Martelli passed on a message from Piero that he didn't like some seraphim the artist had added. Gozzoli responded spiritedly that "they are quite appropriate," and Martelli backed him up, reporting to Piero that "they are nothing to make a fuss about." However, having sent word to Piero that "I will do what you tell me to; two little clouds will take them away," Gozzoli added: "I think that in the coming week I shall have covered all the area I can reach from this scaffolding, and I think you should come and look at it before I take the scaffolding down . . . I am continually looking for ways to do something which will satisfy you, at least in the main."[70]

Apparently, Piero did not return to Florence during the summer to see the frescoes, and Gozzoli suggested that, instead, he might visit Piero: "I wanted to come last Sunday to see you, but I was intimidated by the weather . . . it seems to me a thousand years since your magnificence was here to see if you like the work." Whether he saw it, in the end, the patron went with the artist's choice as far as the seraphim were concerned. The Medici and their friends continued to promote and protect Gozzoli. In 1467, Gozzoli wrote to Piero's son Lorenzo, thanking him for intervening on behalf of a member of his workshop accused of a petty crime. "I shall consider this as having been done for me. To offer myself to you or ask what I can do seems to me superfluous, for I belonged to you and your house before this incident occurred . . . Jesus Christ be with you always."

In the same way that patrons called upon friends for political and financial favors for the friends of friends, Piero de' Medici probably helped Antonio Pollaiuolo to win his commissions from Medici friends like the Dietisalvi-Neroni, Pitti, and Martelli. Certainly, Piero protected the artist in his dispute with the *operai* of the Duomo over his payment for some candlesticks, "because he loves Antonio on account of his virtù." Piero's brother, Giovanni, recommended Mino da Fiesole to his friend the Duke of Milan, who in turn sought to obtain a work from Desiderio da Settignano through the intervention of the Medici. Patrons had artists like Neri di Bicci copy works they had seen in the houses of their friends, to whom they in turn recommended the artists they admired most. Nofri d'Agnolo del Brutto's commission of a *Saint Anne with the Virgin and Child*, now in the Uffizi, from Masolino and Masaccio was probably due to his association with Felice Brancacci, his partner in a silk company at the time that these two artists were painting the Brancacci chapel frescoes at the Carmine. Both commissions made great play of the luxurious textiles whose manufacture had enriched their patrons, particularly in the representation of a pair of well-dressed dandies walking together in the Piazza del Carmine (see Figure 2.6).[71]

A number of these associations came to involve affection and trust that endured over many years, like the friendship between Messer Manno Temperani, a leading statesman of the mid-fifteenth century, and the painter Apollonio di Giovanni, whose workshop made manuscript illuminations (see Figure 2.4) and furnished wedding *cassoni* to the lion's share of the Florentine patriciate. In his last will, Temperani asked that below his tomb should be painted "whatever seems appropriate to Apollonio the painter, to whom he entrusts this and in whom he has faith in view of the delightful goodwill and friendship *(benivolenza et amicizia)* that he brought to the home of the testator." That these sentiments were reciprocated is evident from Apollonio's own will, which made Temperani's son, Giovanni, his universal heir.[72]

While Leonardo da Vinci was painting his portrait of Ginevra de' Benci (Figure 2.10), he seems similarly to have become lifelong friends with Ginevra's brother, Giovanni, patron of Filippino Lippi's *Annunciation*, now in Munich, and Cosimo de' Medici's right-hand man in the Medici bank. Some thirty years later they exchanged a map of the world, books, and semiprecious stones. And in Vasari's day, Leonardo's unfinished *Adoration of the Magi,* now in the Uffizi, belonged to Giovanni's son Amerigo; apparently, Leonardo had entrusted it to his father's care.[73]

There exists a most unusual double portrait depicting the painter Filippino Lippi with his longtime patron, Piero del Pugliese, a chapel-holder in Santa Maria del Carmine, for which Filippino Lippi had painted a *Vision of Saint Bernard,* also with a portrait of the donor. Their double portrait (Figure 2.11) has been seen as representing a new type of friendship between patron and artist based on "sincere affection" instead of patronage. This was a distinction Florentines themselves seem to have found both difficult and unnecessary to make, since clearly affection and trust frequently flourished between partners in the production of works of art. Moreover, the question of what this picture tells us about the relationship between Del Pugliese and Lippi is complicated by the fact that the awkward adaptation of Lippi's self-portrait in the Brancacci chapel frescoes was probably not by his hand. The picture, described in a poem by Alessandro Braccesi, seems to be part of the ongoing debate between poets and painters as to which of them could best bring the dead alive and made the absent present and may also refer to Pliny's description of the ideal marriage of minds between patron and artist.[74]

Our exploration of where Florentines met and made friends, and the interests they shared, confirms Aristotle's view of

2.10. Leonardo da Vinci, *Ginevra de' Benci.*

2.11. Filippino Lippi, attributed, portrait of himself with his patron, Piero del Pugliese.

the importance of quotidian association in fostering friendships among *vicini,* men of differing social status but literally
"nearest" one another in the neighborhood, secular or spiritual, of the *gonfalone* or the parish, the street corner, church,
or work place, and who in the course of everyday life traced
the same itineraries through the city, orchestrated by the
sound of the same church and municipal bells.[75]

Friends from the neighborhood, be it urban or rural, including men and women of all classes, were particularly visible around the baptismal font (Figure 2.12). Like other forms
of friendship, the relationships created or expressed by godparentage combined familiarity with advantage. They involved elaborate mutual obligations, including favors, protection, and gift giving, between spiritual parents and birth
parents, as well as their children. So the choice of godparents,
like that of marriage partners, presented an opportunity to
procure political allies and pursue social strategies. It was
common for men to make collective godparents or co-fathers
of a group with whom they held public office. When his first
son was born, Piero de' Medici invited all his fellow members
of the Signoria to be godparents to Lorenzo, and Gregorio
Dati gave a son no less than thirteen godfathers by naming almost all his fellow standard-bearers of the *gonfalone* in which
he lived.[76]

However, the majority of godparents were people with
whom the child's parents daily did business or shared pleasures. Giovanni Morelli, whose godparents were all from his
father's parish, advised his sons to honor their friends and

neighbors by inviting them to dinner or by baptizing their children. Godparentage clearly followed the course of neighborhood sociability in the case of Bartolomeo Masi, the coppersmith who was a member of half a dozen companies dedicated to pleasure, particularly dining, and was named as a godparent forty-eight times by fellow artisans.[77] The same was true of the relationship between the miniaturist Filippo Torelli and Francesco di Bivigliano degli Alberti, who was godfather to Torelli's son. Alberti explained in a letter to Piero de' Medici that Torelli "has a farm a stone's throw from mine and every day we chat together."[78]

Of the thirty-four godparents the wool merchant Matteo Corsini chose for his children, half were from his parish of San Felice in Piazza, and most of the others came either from his *gonfalone* or were his neighbors in the countryside. They included his notary, the daughter of a business partner, a fellow guildsman who acted as witness to his notarial acts, and his principal supplier of stationery. Similarly, Marco Parenti chose as godfather to one of his children the bookseller Vespasiano da Bisticci, from whom he procured illuminated manuscripts of Aristotle's and Cicero's letters.[79] A high proportion of godparents were men, with whom fathers were more likely to associate in business or pleasure, or to mutual advantage. However, the church prescribed at least one godmother, and Corsini named as "spiritual mothers" to his children the wives of neighborhood tradesmen or poor neighborhood widows, "for the love of God," meaning that it was

2.12. The font in the Baptistery, Florence.

they who were the recipients of gifts, making the nomination of godparents another form of charity.[80]

Where most forms of friendship flourished between individual males or groups of men, the "spiritual friendships" created by godparentage could involve whole families. The neighbors who held at the font the children of Cambio di Tano Petrucci, a goldsmith resident in the *gonfalone* of the Red Lion and the parish of San Pancrazio, included the notary he frequented, Ser Tommaso Carondini, Carondini's wife, Mea, and also his mother. The cobbler Antonio di Ciecho, from whom Petrucci bought his shoes, also took part in the baptism of most of his children, and a daughter born in 1409 was "given to God" by the doublet maker Manno di Bonuccio di Manno, who was standard-bearer of the *gonfalone* of the Red Lion in 1427.[81]

"Spiritual fathers," as those who "made Christians" of their friends' children, were part of the patriarchal hierarchy that joined heaven and earth. It was their responsibility to "give the child to God" and to oversee its instruction in the faith. The godchild was obligated to honor the godfather; as San Bernardino explained in his sermons: "The first father is eternal God. The second father is your natural father. The third father is your godfather."[82] Friendship between Florentines was framed once again in Christian terms by the act of holding a child at the font. The very stones of hell reminded Dante of "those in my beautiful San Giovanni, made for the baptizers to stand on," and when he met his ancestor Cacciaguida in heaven, Dante had him extol the fellowship Florentines enjoyed through baptism into this Christian community: "To such a peaceful, such a pleasant/civic life, to such a trusty/body of citizens, to such a sweet abode,/ Mary gave me, called on with loud cries,/and in your ancient Baptistery,/I became at once a Christian, and Cacciaguida."[83]

# THREE

# Could Friends Be Trusted?

$\mathcal{T}$HIS chapter turns from the meaning of friendship and the manner of its making to focus on the issue of fidelity. Could friends be trusted? The answer was no, or hardly ever, according to Giovanni Morelli, a wary Florentine merchant whose *Ricordi* (memoirs) constitute a manual for his heirs on social self-defense. He thought it wise to "test your friend a hundred times . . . before you trust him once." He stressed that protestations of eternal fidelity were invariably suspect and added that "you should never trust anyone so much that he can destroy you."[1]

If Morelli's fears border on the paranoid, they nevertheless reflect a widespread anxiety arising from the real tensions and conflicts that pervaded this society. Visions of betrayal by friends were always before Florentine eyes. There were numerous examples in the city's tumultuous political life, and even in the central events of the Christian story, from which men learned how to regard human nature. On the altars or the walls of churches they saw paintings reminding them of the testing of Saint Peter, who failed in loyalty by denying his friendship with Jesus, not once but thrice, and of how the disciples slept in the garden of Gethsemane while their Lord, in the agony of contemplating his imminent Passion, exclaimed "could you not watch with me one hour?" The figure of Judas, the dearly loved disciple who betrayed Christ with a kiss, was as vivid in the minds of ordinary Florentines as it is in Giotto's representation of this scene, in his frescoes depicting the life of Christ in the Arena Chapel in Padua (Figure 3.1).[2]

As Cosimo de' Medici observed, "A man's deeds best commend his intentions." The acid test of friendship, love, and trust was in action. This chapter looks at groups of friends at moments of crisis or trial, in which friendships were tested and either failed or endured. Most of the friends considered here were prominent statesmen who were supporters of the Medici. They were the sort of men whose relationships Cicero envisaged in his *De Amicitia*, in which he raised the question of potential conflicts between loyalty to friends and loyalty to the state, asking how far men should go for love of their friends and concluding, rather idealistically, that it was impossible to imagine virtuous men importuning friends for anything "contrary to good faith . . . or the public good *(rem publicam)*." Aristotle, indeed, saw such friendships

3.1. Giotto da Bondone, *Judas Betrays Christ with a Kiss*, fresco, Arena Chapel, Padua.

as the best defense against civil hatreds, because they were the links that bound the city together. But when they failed, they could also tear it apart, a process that Dante made the major theme of his *Inferno*. Among the Medici friends, it was their leading partisans who, when it came to the crunch, were in a position to destroy—or save—them.[3]

In July 1463, a fourteen-year-old Lorenzo de' Medici wrote to his father, Piero, announcing that his party had arrived in Pistoia and been well received there by his kinsman the Archbishop, Donato de' Medici, and "by all the people of this place." He went on to express his desire, "because we are in the middle of a *festa* and are eager to see what lies on the road further ahead," to press on to Lucca and Pisa. "We beg you, therefore, that it may please you to satisfy us by giving us your immediate permission, and to obtain it we are sending this servant, by whom may it please you to write to us that you are agreeable." As he ingeniously concluded: "If you do not reply, we will interpret your lack of an answer as a quick way of giving your consent." The letter was signed "your sons, Lorenzo de' Medici, Braccio Martelli, Sigismondo della Stufa, and Ser Francesco." (The last of Piero's honorary sons was his younger brother Giovanni's secretary, Francesco Cantansanti, who accompanied the boys as companion and chaperone).[4]

Arguably, the most significant experience that lay ahead for these young friends, fifteen years further on down the road, was the conspiracy of the papacy and the Pazzi family with their Salviati relatives, allies once among the oldest and most trusted of the Medici *amici.* The conspirators hoped to overthrow the Medici family's political leadership and ruin their bank by assassinating Lorenzo and his younger brother, Giuliano, as they stood during Mass before the high altar of Florence Cathedral (Figure 3.2). This was the same setting, again packed with people, in which, almost forty years earlier, "the whole city" had pondered the gap between ideal and actual friendship.

In the events of Sunday April 26, 1478, as described by the poet Poliziano and in the diary of Marco Parenti's son Piero, all the familiar rituals of friendship—the visit, the dinner, the embrace, and the meeting in church—were enacted and their meaning inverted in the subsequent betrayal. The occasion of the plot was Cardinal Raffaello Riario Sansoni's visit to Florence. Invoking the obligations of friends to offer hospitality, the conspirators encouraged Lorenzo to prepare a banquet for the visitors at the Medici palace. When word came that their guests had arrived, Lorenzo and Giuliano, who had gone to the cathedral a hundred yards away to hear Mass, returned home to greet them, accompanied by a large number of other citizens wishing to honor the visitors. The entire party then returned to Santa Maria del Fiore, one of the conspirators walking arm-in-arm with Lorenzo.[5]

At this point, the plan to carry out the murder during the meal was altered to accomplish it under cover of the enormous crowd in the church. The assassins took up their posi-

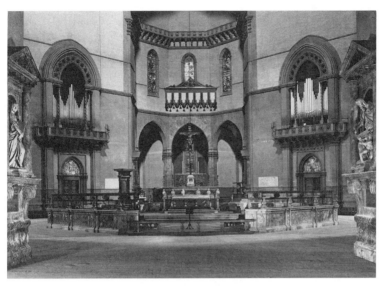

3.2. Cathedral of Florence, view of high altar and north and south sacristies.

tions around the choir, sticking closely to Giuliano while he chatted with Giovanni Tornabuoni and Francesco Nori, who were, as Parenti observed, "two of the principle directors of their business." At a prearranged signal, some said the priest's elevation of the host, they drew their swords. Giuliano was slain, but Lorenzo was only wounded. A group of friends hustled him to safety behind the bronze doors of the north sacristy. Francesco Nori, a partner of the Medici bank who had tried to get between Giuliano and his attackers to defend him, was run through the stomach with a sword. Still breathing, he was carried into the sacristy, where he died.[6]

Among the friends who huddled with Lorenzo in the sacristy, recently and sumptuously redecorated by Giuliano da Maiano (Figure 3.3), were Braccio Martelli, Sigismondo della Stufa, and the poet Poliziano. In Poliziano's words:

A group of young men faithful to the Medici were gathering with their weapons outside the sacristy doors. They shouted that they were all friends or relatives of Lorenzo and that he should come out before his enemies became stronger. We inside were anxious, not knowing if these were friends or enemies, and asked if Giuliano were alone. To this they answered nothing. Then Sigismondo della Stufa, a valiant young man, bound to Lorenzo by many ties of love and duty since childhood, went up the stairs to where the organ was and hurried to a small window that looked out into the church. When he saw the body of Giuliano lying there he understood what evil had transpired. He saw that those who were waiting outside the door were friends, and he ordered the doors opened. They took Lorenzo in the midst of a group of armed men and led him home so that he should not come upon the corpse of his brother.[7]

The Pazzi conspiracy involved factors far beyond the scope of our focus on friendship and its betrayal. Lorenzo's misuse of Florentine law and diplomacy to protect his personal interests was clearly a crucial issue.[8] After Giuliano had fallen, Iacopo Salviati rode to the Piazza della Signoria shouting the republican slogan: "The people and liberty!" Later, Alamanno Rinuccini's *De Libertate* represented Giuliano's murder as an act against tyranny.[9] Economic rivalry was also an obvious motive. By 1457, the leaders of the Medici family were the city's highest taxpayers, far ahead of any others. But two Pazzi households, those of Iacopo di Messer Andrea and the sons of his brother Antonio, were among the top ten taxpayers, and their combined wealth exceeded that of any other family except the Medici. In 1474, Pope Sixtus IV transferred his principal business from the Medici bank to that of Iacopo de' Pazzi, with far-reaching consequences, not only for the friendship between the two families, but also for the Florentine state's relations with other major political players on the peninsula.[10]

As far as friendship is concerned, the Pazzi conspiracy was merely the most dramatic demonstration in fifteenth-century Florence of the propensity of friendships involving patronage to sour into enmity when they ceased to serve the *onore et utile* (the honor and profit) of both parties. The Medici

3.3. Cathedral of Florence, interior of north sacristy, view through the open door to the high altar.

motto *semper* (always), symbolized by a diamond ring, was merely wishful thinking. As Anselmo Calderoni, herald to the Signoria, had observed in 1441 at the *certame coronario,* friendships were inherently volatile, "turning, like the leaves,/as the whim strikes us,/sometimes for desire and sometimes for disdain."[11] Over the century, the dynamic between the Medici and their most powerful friends changed. Cosimo had earned his authority over his peers. The "succession" of Piero and a very young Lorenzo to his position as head of the Medici party and its expansion to embrace an ever-larger proportion of the city led its leaders, old friends who felt their interests neglected, to believe they might be better served by other patrons and friends.[12]

The friendship between the Pazzi and Medici families was originally based on close personal and commercial relations, which went back at least to the 1420s. In these years, the junior managers of the Rome bank of Cosimo's cousin Averardo were Averado's son, Giuliano, and Andrea di Guglielmino de' Pazzi, who was married to a daughter of Alamanno Salviati, one of Averardo's sons-in-law. At this time, Florence was financing its war with Lucca largely with citizen loans, especially from the Officials of the Bank. The members of this office included Cosimo, the commune's biggest creditor, who loaned the enormous sum of 156,000 florins, and Andrea de' Pazzi, the second largest lender, who loaned almost 60,000 florins. Averardo de' Medici and his son, Giuliano, died in exile in 1434, when the leaders of the Medici family were expelled from Florence; the personal intimacy, which was the basis of trust, between the two families may have died with them.[13] The alliance persisted for another forty years, and like that of the Medici, the Pazzi bank continued to be spectacularly successful. Personal evidence about the Pazzi family is sparse, but it seems that the Medici did not promote them politically as much as their wealth might have led them to expect.[14]

Although the friendship between the Pazzi and the Medici remained strong at the time of Andrea's death in 1445, he had notably been among the first of the Medici *amici* whose artistic patronage, in its scale and nature, might suggest rivalry as much as emulation. Adjacent to the church of Santa Croce, Andrea built a chapel, designed by Brunelleschi, which was almost a carbon copy of Brunelleschi's Old Sacristy at San Lorenzo, commissioned in the 1420s by Cosimo's father, Giovanni di Bicci de' Medici, as his burial chapel. The Pazzi palace was similarly, if more complexly, related stylistically to the earlier Medici palace.[15]

Cosimo, obviously aware that the Pazzi posed a potential threat to his family's supremacy, had arranged a marriage in 1459 between his granddaughter Bianca and Andrea's grandson Guglielmo, a prominent figure in the circle of Lorenzo's young friends. In that year, when Lorenzo was ten, two members of the Pazzi family, Renato di Pietro and Giovanni d'Antonio, were among the solidly Medicean group of twelve youths who were chosen to stage a joust for the visit of Galeazzo Maria Sforza, son of Cosimo's major foreign ally, the Duke of Milan. Guglielmo traveled with Lorenzo to Rome in 1465, and in 1469 returned there, along with Giuliano de' Medici, as one of the band of youths who went to fetch Lorenzo's bride, Clarice Orsini, and bring her back with them to Florence.[16]

According to Poliziano's account of the conspiracy, Gugliemo knew about it, and was "thought to sit, as it is said, in two saddles." After the event, "trusting in his family ties, [he] found refuge in Lorenzo's palace." He and all his sons, Lorenzo's nephews, were later exiled, but only to a distance of some twenty miles from the city.[17] The case of Guglielmo de' Pazzi shows that far from being the simple confrontation between friends and enemies of the Medici presented in Poliziano's self-consciously literary account, based heavily on Sallust's *Cataline Conspiracy*, the Pazzi conspiracy, which left many Florentines shocked and shaken, exposed the extreme complexity of personal relationships among intertwined relatives and friends.

Those friends who remained faithful, proving their personal devotion and loyalty to Lorenzo in standing by him literally to the death, were bound to him, as Poliziano noted, by ties of "love and duty" in friendships that combined pleasure and profit with virtue and embraced erotic, as well as Neo-platonic, love. Five of the ten brothers of the main Martelli household in the mid-fifteenth century served as partners or managers of the Medici bank. Both the Martelli and Della Stufa families had been neighborhood allies of the Medici since the mid-fourteenth century. In the 1340s, when the nobles took up arms against the people, those of the quarter of

San Giovanni chose as their leaders "the Medici and the Rondinelli and Messer Ugo della Stufa, a judge." In 1434, after Cosimo's enemies failed to oppose his recall from exile by force, a disgruntled group of armed men set fire to the Martelli houses. Like Francesco Nori, who became the owner of one of the most richly appointed palaces of the era when the will of its builder, Alberto di Zanobi, was set aside by a special law passed with the support of leading Mediceans, these families had derived a great deal of *utile* (profit)—seen by some as inimical to true friendship—from their association with their Medici friends and patrons, by whom they were protected and favored in business, politics, and their personal desires.[18]

Within the firm supporting framework of this patronage, Lorenzo's boyhood attachments, of the sort that Cicero described in his *De Amicitia* as often cast aside like outgrown garments, endured into maturity.[19] A wide range of the shared experience that we have seen to be the firmest foundation of Florentine friendship had reinforced the bonds between Lorenzo, Sigismondo della Stufa, and Braccio Martelli between the days of their country jaunt in 1463 and what even a Medici critic like Piero Parenti described as "the horrible and terrifying incident in our city of the death of Giuliano de' Medici."[20]

Living in the family palaces that stood within a stone's throw of one another (see Figure 2.3), these youths were in and out of one another's houses and the church of San Lorenzo (Figure 3.4). As chapel-holders and sophisticated

3.4. Church of San Lorenzo, Florence, view of nave and crossing.

patrons of their parish church, the families cooperated in the church's renovation in the classical style, according to Brunelleschi's plan. Crucial to this plan was the enlarging of the piazza in front of the Della Stufa houses. That was accomplished in April 1434, while the Medici were in exile in Venice, by Lotteringho d'Andrea della Stufa, then serving on the Signoria. Lotteringho's nephew Ugo di Lorenzo della Stufa, Sigismondo's father, wrote to the young Lorenzo de' Medici's uncle, Giovanni di Cosimo, noting "all the brotherhood which has existed between us," and describing how "the houses opposite ours have been levelled, so that now there is a beautiful piazza in front of the door."[21] To embellish the church, for the love and glory of God, the honor of the city, and the commemoration of themselves, these families worked together and with leading artists, who were also friends, among them Filippo Lippi, Donatello, Desiderio da Settignano, and Verrocchio.[22]

A letter to Cosimo de' Medici from a mutual friend described Domenico Martelli as "a fine and wise man, very tender and loving to his friends."[23] The letters to Lorenzo from Domenico's son Braccio, and from Sigismondo della Stufa, illuminate many aspects of the love between friends, including the erotic. On one occasion, Braccio Martelli wrote to Lorenzo "to tell you what has happened since you left . . . I have chosen to offer you a somewhat bitter pleasure rather than remain silent about our happiness . . ." Apologizing for the roughness of his writing, Braccio suggested that even "the eloquence of Giovanni Boccaccio, the divine narrator of similar events, might not suffice" to describe the joys of an evening spent singing and dancing with some beautiful women, and how "our hands, touching such delicacy trembled, and stunned by our feelings, refused to carry out their function." After another such night, Braccio and his friends rode hell for leather through the grain fields "without any regard or consideration for drenching ourselves, so that we would have been no less sodden if we had passed through the middle of the Arno, and finally arrived, wet on the outside and burning within, to the desired place, where we had, honestly, the greatest pleasures . . . until the sixth hour of the night."[24]

Lorenzo and his youthful companions participated enthusiastically in the games and ceremonies associated with the courtly and neo-feudal culture that flourished in Laurentian Florence. In 1469, Lorenzo fought the customary joust, which he dedicated not to Clarice Orsini, his Roman bride of several months, but to the object of his ideal love, Lucrezia Donati.[25] That same year, Sigismondo della Stufa wrote to him of an encounter with Lucrezia in the church of Santissima Annunziata in terms at once idealizing and very down to earth: "You never saw anything so beautiful, dressed in black and with her head veiled, stepping so gracefully that it was as if the very stones and walls should worship her as she passed. I will say no more, lest you be tempted by sin in this holy season."[26] Even lustier was Braccio Martelli's letter to Lorenzo graphically describing the party at which Niccolò Ardinghelli, whose prodigious sexual equipment he compared to a "bull's horn," deflowered his future wife while his friend Martelli stood guard.[27] A question that arises here is "who was watching whom, and why?," especially when we learn that at another of the group's parties, Braccio and other men appeared in women's dress. Braccio was indicted several times for acts of sodomy, which allegedly took place in the Martelli palace or stable, and once involved a servant of Sigismondo della Stufa's father, Agnolo, although all those named were eventually absolved of blame.[28]

The Medici regime under Lorenzo was relatively tolerant of homosexual behavior; not surprising, when one reads Lorenzo's erotic poetry, built upon elaborate double entendre, which might in modern times be described as polymorphous perversity.[29] Not long after Lorenzo's death, Niccolò di Tribolo, known as Jacone, one of the circle of artists around Michelangelo whose talents the Medici had nurtured, produced a drawing of two seated naked men touching hands with the inscription in the artist's hand, "Some say it is better to take a wife"; this should probably be read as a homoerotic joke (Figure 3.5).[30] It was not until the early sixteenth century, however, that an artist depicted a friend as an alluring object. Raphael's formal portrait of his friend Bindo Altoviti, a beautiful Florentine banker (Figure 3.6), represented him as an ideal male beauty, to be admired by his wife or other friends, such as the bisexual Michelangelo, who used Altoviti's bank to send remittances from Rome to Florence, and who gave the banker his preparatory cartoon for the Sistine ceiling scene of *The Drunkenness of Noah*.[31]

At the same time, the youthful *brigata* of Lorenzo's friends, including Antonio de' Pazzi, was the major audience for Marsilio Ficino's Neoplatonic writings, which elevated friendship and erotic love as pathways to Divine love. They were among the chief recipients of Ficino's letters recommending the application of these doctrines to practical personal and civic problems. Ficino, a proven and trusted friend of the Medici, who had grown up around their household because his father had been Cosimo's doctor, wrote to Lorenzo of the great longing of friends to communicate and spend time together, and assured Giuliano that a friend is always within a friend.[32] The concept of love expressed by Lorenzo in his *Comment on His own Sonnets* derives directly from Ficino's idea that the rational soul of man is possessed of the capacity to unite the finite with the infinite. As he wrote to Ficino of their friendship: "You belong not to Marsilio, but to your Lorenzo, who is no less yours than you are yours . . . Often you have revealed your mind to me, but in this letter you have gone beyond every duty of friendship. Others in their goodwill offer the gifts of riches, honor or pleasure. But you are such a fount of instruction . . . that for this you are the first among my friends in virtue and before everyone in love."[33]

Giuliano's ideal beloved, Simonetta Vespucci, to whom he dedicated his joust of 1475, and who died of consumption a year before his murder, was memorialized in the verses his friend Poliziano wrote on the theme of the joust. Simonetta has been identified as the subject of an idealized portrait attributed to Botticelli, an artist closely associated with the

3.5. Niccolò di Tribolo, known as "Jacone," *Two Seated Men,* drawing.

3.6. Raphael Sanzio, *Bindo Altoviti.*

Medici whose paintings, particularly the *Primavera (Spring)* embodied the spirit of the culture of the Laurentian circle.[34] When Sigismondo della Stufa's fiancée, Albiera degli Albizzi, died at the age of fifteen in August 1473, on the very eve of their wedding, Ficino wrote reminding him that "the soul is the man himself and the body but his shadow . . . You will only cease to weep, Gismondo, when you cease looking for your Albiera degli Albizzi in her dark shadow and begin to follow her by her own clear light. For the further she is from that misshapen shadow the more beautiful you will find her, past all you have ever known."[35] Her marble bust is known to us only from an inscription recorded in a poem dedicated "To the Marble Bust of Albiera, whose noble form is to be admired . . . Lest there be on earth any lovelier than the goddesses,/Death, at the command of the deities, carried me off." Albiera's bust may have resembled the one by Verrocchio, similar to many others in its tone and general attributes, that some have seen as a portrait of Lucrezia Donati. Verrocchio certainly painted the banner bearing Lucrezia's image that Lorenzo carried into his joust in 1469.[36]

The representation of the Pazzi conspiracy by poets and artists in the Medici circle of friends, like the representations of their friendships, combined passion, propaganda, and idealization. Botticelli's posthumous portrait of Giuliano (Figure 3.7) maintained the martyr's presence before Medici sympathizers, while the subject's lowered eyes, the open door, and the redbreasted bird poignantly referred to death and the hope of resurrection. Unfortunately, Filippino Lippi's copy of Botticelli's drawing of a hanged man is the only trace of Botticelli's commission from the police magistracy to depict the defeated and disgraced conspirators on the facade of the Bargello, the city's court house.[37]

The medal that Lorenzo commissioned to commemorate the Pazzi conspiracy may be seen as the visual counterpart of Poliziano's narrative. It was made by Bertoldo di Giovanni, the favored sculptor who lived in the Medici palace and was described by contemporaries as one whom Lorenzo "loved as much as any of his *familiari*;" he may have been portrayed in Botticelli's painting of a young man holding a medal of Cosimo de' Medici (Figure 3.8). Radically original in form and function, Bertoldo's medal recalled Cosimo's close friend Donatello's work, which was considered to be one of the glories of Florence. It was the first widely circulated medal to serve as a memorial to a living member of the Medici family. The medal's inscriptions, "public grief" beneath the portrait of Giuliano and "public safety" beneath that of Lorenzo, carry a clear propagandistic message idealizing the Medici regime, presenting Giuliano as a martyr to the republic and Lorenzo as its savior (Figure 3.9).[38]

The Pazzi conspiracy was widely seen as ending the joyful springtime of Lorenzo's circle, from which the sweet bird of youth had inexorably flown. However, the ambivalence of its members' relationships, including at least the temporary estrangement of both Poliziano and Ficino from their Medici friends, extended even to the brothers themselves.[39] While Braccio Martelli claimed that Lorenzo had no greater friend

3.7. Sandro Botticelli, *Giuliano de' Medici,* posthumous portrait.

3.8. Sandro Botticelli, *Young Man Holding a Medal of Cosimo de' Medici*, possibly a portrait of Lorenzo's friend, the sculptor Bertoldo di Giovanni.

3.9. Bertoldo di Giovanni, bronze medal commemorating the Pazzi conspiracy, 1478.

than his younger brother, Giuliano confided to the Milanese ambassador that "he knew very well that Lorenzo didn't want him known to the world, nor that he should have any reputation," and in a letter written several years after Giuliano's death, Piero Vespucci told Lucrezia Tornabuoni, mother of Giuliano and Lorenzo, that "[Giuliano] told me many times that he was the least happy young man, not just of Florence, but of all Italy."[40]

The Pazzi conspiracy had literally demonstrated the truth of another popular Florentine dictum about friendship: "one enemy can harm you more than four friends can help you."[41] In the later fifteenth century, the eccentric Benedetto Dei, merchant, Medici spy, and an inveterate measurer and recorder of the attributes of his city and its inhabitants, kept a balance sheet of friends and enemies, listing his "heartfelt enemies" in his *Chronicle* alongside his "proven friends."[42] In view of the volatility of social configurations sensitive to political as well as personal events, keeping account of these constantly changing relationships was an essential survival strategy.

The first great fifteenth-century test of friendships among members of the Florentine ruling class had been Cosimo de' Medici's exile by his enemies in September 1433. The anti-Mediceans were exiled, in their turn, after Cosimo's repatriation in September 1434, along with those former familiars who had failed this test of friendship, usually considered in this essentially political context as partisanship. The personal letters containing protestations of loyalty addressed to Medici family members in the year of their exile and shortly after their return help to define the inner circle of Medici friends and supporters. But personal friendship and political partisanship did not perfectly coincide. This gap may be measured by the letters from erstwhile friends to Cosimo in the weeks between his recall by the Signoria that took office on September 1st and the pronouncement a couple of months later of most of the sentences of exile against his enemies.[43]

Those ultimately banished comprised nearly a hundred individuals from fifty-eight families, among them the leading households of the city's largest lineage, the Strozzi, and including its wealthiest and most influential member, the admired, respected, learned, and relatively apolitical knight, Messer Palla di Nofri. Many Medici partisans were also friends of Palla di Nofri Strozzi and considered his proscription an act of great injustice. For the next four decades, the Medici regime refused to consider his repatriation from Padua, where he eventually died at the age of seventy-three. This intransigence came back to haunt the Medici in the form of the conspiracy against Piero in 1466, when a group of leading Mediceans who notably had remained close to the Strozzi family rose up to oppose Medici supremacy in the name of freedom and justice.[44]

The language of fidelity and trust common to friendship and patronage renders them indistinguishable in Cosimo's own memoir of the events of 1433–34. <u>He attributed the survival of his bank, the essential foundation of his power and authority, to the failure of his enemies to undermine the trust *(fede)* of its clients</u>. This he ascribed, along with all the prosperity he subsequently enjoyed, "to the goodwill *(benivolenza)* and shrewd operations of my [faithful] friends *(amici)*," still a relatively small group of men tightly bound to him by close personal as well as political ties and by quotidian association *(usanza)*.[45]

There is clearer evidence of personal intimacy in the relationships of Cosimo and his brother, Lorenzo, with the humanists Poggio Bracciolini and Niccolò Niccoli, based on a shared passion for the recovery and spread of classical learning. The Medici brothers joined Poggio and Niccoli in the hunt for classical manuscripts and in the campaign to create libraries for the convents of San Marco and the Badia, and traveled with them to search for inscriptions in the ruins of Ostia Antica. Nevertheless, at the death of his friends' father, Giovanni di Bicci de' Medici, Poggio was uncertain how to describe him, bemoaning the loss of "such a good and delightful friend, although I ought to say patron." In 1433, he wrote to Niccoli: "I heard of the fall of our Cosmus with misery and with the deepest regret, but such is the state of our times that keeping quiet is safer, though less honorable."[46] Not necessarily easier to interpret in terms of personal relations is the opposite reaction of Piero Ginori, a longtime Medici friend and supporter, who on hearing the news of Cosimo's arrest, "quite fearlessly roamed the city, shouting out, and showing himself to be utterly lacking in wisdom."[47]

On the other hand, Ambrogio Traversari, Prior of the convent of Santa Maria degli Angeli, where the Medici brothers spent many hours attending learned symposia, wrote in his *Hodoeporicon* that their exile "seemed to me a nightmare," the danger they were in "an endless anguish to me," and that "I fell into a profound depression . . . at the misfortune of these two great friends." He also took action, intervening on their behalf with the Venetian government and even appealing to their archrival, Rinaldo degli Albizzi, who had led the coup against them. Ambrogio traveled to Bologna in order to snatch a moment with Lorenzo, who was on his way into exile in Venice, and was moved to tears when he visited Cosimo in custody in the palace of the Signoria. The same mixture of intellectual friendship, partisan affiliation, and an intense personal attachment is evident in letters from other Medici friends in this period.[48]

It is clear from the letters written by the silk merchant Felice Brancacci to Cosimo in late 1434 and in 1435 concerning Felice's exile, along with his Strozzi friends and in-laws, that both Felice and Cosimo felt their trust in one another had been betrayed. The iconography of the frescoes for the Brancacci family chapel in Santa Maria del Carmine, painted in the later 1420s by Masaccio and Masolino, suggests that even before the patron was expelled from Florence, like Adam and Eve from the Garden of Eden, he was preoccupied with trust, as fundamental to friendship as it was to marriages and business contracts, underpinning public order and private virtue. Scenes of the *Temptation* of mankind's father and mother and their expulsion after the *Fall* frame the cycle of scenes from the life of Saint Peter, with its messages of trust betrayed and trust redeemed, through charity, faith, and the fulfillment of responsibilities to the community.[49]

The contact of hands in several scenes seals crucial personal and social contracts: those of Saint Peter and the tax collector to whom he gives the tribute money (Figure 3.10) and those of Saint Peter and the poor woman to whom he gives alms (Figure 3.11). An unusual scene in this Petrine cycle is the elevation of Saint Peter on a throne; the description in a popular explication of the liturgy of the feast day to celebrate this event describes Peter as freeing men from three kinds of sins: "our sins against, God, our neighbors, and ourselves." Felice's betrayal of all three of these by embezzling a large sum of money entrusted to his care as treasurer of the communal Camera was a subtext of his friendship with Cosimo, from whom he borrowed the money to repay the commune.[50]

Nevertheless, in his forensic analysis of their once-close friendship, Felice referred repeatedly to his own fidelity by contrast with Cosimo's betrayal of his faith. On September 18, 1434, ten days before Cosimo was recalled to Florence, Felice had written to him in Venice, addressing him as "honored brother" and explaining that he had not replied earlier to his friend's letters "so as not to enter into a conspiracy against the state" (communication with exiles was itself a crime). Now, he was moved to write, with a mixture of self-criticism and self-justification, "with the intention of ameliorating your woes and the excuses of the regime and especially my own . . .:

> And yet in your letter there are words that seem spoken with the intention of blaming me, which I would rather not believe you used for that reason. But I want it settled between us, that before the Palace (the Priors) suspected you, I never did or sought anything that would harm you . . . I conformed to the government's view, so that I have nothing to ask your pardon for. So do not threaten me that you will never forgive me . . . And I should tell you that I have gone to confession twice or more, and also taken communion, and as yet I have not asked forgiveness of you . . . I never offended against our friendship, which has lasted for almost thirty years with such . . . straightforwardness on your part and mine as if we were monks in the same order."[51]

Felice continued to address Cosimo as an intimate personal friend. Even after Cosimo was elected Gonfalonier of Justice and became the official head of government, Felice confessed, adjuring him to secrecy, "that to save you the trouble of defending my person, despite my innocence, for the benefit of others I have proceeded secretly to Siena, and no-one in Florence knows this except yourself and one other, and I am hiding here until I hear what is decided about me."[52]

At the same time, Felice reproached Cosimo for allowing partisanship to triumph over friendship and trust:

3.10. Masaccio, *The Tribute Money*, detail of Saint Peter paying the tax collector, fresco, Brancacci Chapel, Florence.

3.11. Masaccio, *Distribution of Goods*, detail of Saint Peter giving alms to a poor woman, Brancacci Chapel, Florence.

When I consider what I saw you do to that knight [Palla Strozzi] to save yourself, and I saw you give your hand *(impalmarsi)* and your word *(fede)* to more than six of the Priors for your own freedom . . . and now I see him exiled, and with scorn heaped upon him, his exile increased . . . then I suffer my own situation more patiently . . . given that I always made it clear that you were never to blame and that you couldn't have done anything else, and although I must say that these words made a fool of me, nevertheless, I maintain this faith.[53]

In his last extant letter to Cosimo, dated June 1437, signed "your *(tuo)* Felice recommends himself to you, as you have taught me to say," recriminations had given way to reflection. "Many times I have taken up my pen to respond to your letter and said to myself, 'Why take the trouble to make yourself more hateful than you are, or rather to write things contrary to truth and to your own inclination?'" Touching only briefly on the rights and wrongs of Cosimo's actions since his return from exile, Felice averred that he himself "always acted in such a manner that I never conspired either with those inside the city or outside it. I would prefer to constitute a new party favoring the well-being of my *patria*, had I the confidence *(credito)* and concurrence of men who desire what I do." But he refused to repudiate his friendship with Cosimo:

Since you deny me your aid, at least don't deny me your advice. And if ever during our friendship I did anything that deserved any reward, although I remain more your debtor than your creditor . . . now give me your trusty advice, and without threat to me in your words, for in my opinion you are obliged to me for only one thing, and that is that in your difficulty I was a faithful friend to you, if a little timid out of fear for myself.[54]

The conflicting expectations of Florentine friendships among members of the ruling class are further illuminated by the breakdown of relations in the late 1450s and early 1460s between the Medici and four of their "very closest friends": Luca Pitti, Dietisalvi di Nerone Neroni, Niccolò Soderini, and above all, Agnolo Acciaiuoli, one of Cosimo's original friends and partisans who had been exiled along with the Medici in 1433. These men were among those most tightly bound to the family, and themselves the Medici party's most powerful and trusty lieutenants, in whose hands much of its influence was concentrated. These friendships were weakened by personal rivalry and ambition and finally destroyed by loyalties divided, between the Medici and other friends, particularly of the Strozzi circle, and by political principles many Florentines thought the Medici had betrayed.

By the third quarter of the fifteenth century, Florence was governed essentially by the private agreements of a group of Medici friends. The duty many leading citizens felt to the republic sometimes conflicted with the debt of fidelity owed to friends, which Aristotle believed would bind cities together.[55]

The growing conviction of the conspirators of 1466 that they could lead the Medicean party more ably than Cosimo and his elder son, Piero, was frankly expressed in their correspondence with Francesco Sforza, Duke of Milan. Sforza was Florence's most important foreign ally; since the early 1430s, he had also been a close personal friend of Cosimo, who shared his fascination with the minutiae of war and military strategies.

In the last years of Cosimo's life, Acciaiuoli and Dietisalvi, in particular, sought to replace him in Sforza's esteem as spokesmen for the Florentine state. In a letter to Sforza in 1463, Acciaiuoli described Cosimo and Piero as "men grown cold, whom illness and old age have reduced to such cowardice that they avoid anything that might cause them exertion or trouble . . . they are more timid than rabbits, because they are ill and don't want to displease anyone." To his son, Iacopo, Acciaiuoli confided that "the affairs of our government could not be in worse order or more badly governed. Cosimo and Piero remain in bed and do what they can, but they can't do what is necessary for the city."[56]

Acciaiuoli's letters of the 1460s to family and friends, both before and after his participation in the "conspiracy" of 1466 against Piero, reveal how deeply he was embedded not only in the Medici friendship network, comprising men like the Martelli, Ginori, and Dietisalvi-Neroni, but also in the circle of Strozzi friends and allies. Some of these, like Palla Strozzi and the Brancacci, were in exile; others, like Giovanni Rucellai and the exiled Matteo Strozzi's widow, Alessandra

Strozzi, lived in Florence. Acciauoli was closely involved in the attempt at this time to repatriate Alessandra's sons, Filippo and Lorenzo, who were attempting to repair the family fortunes with their flourishing business in Naples. The Acciaiuoli had ties with Naples stretching back to the mid-fourteenth century, when the family had been feudatories in the Holy Land of the King of Naples, and Nicola Acciaiuoli had served him as seneschal. Agnolo told his own son, Iacopo, how tightly they were bound to Filippo Strozzi and what an injustice the Florentine government had done him, and he expressed the hope that while it was impossible at present to assist him, the time might come when things would be arranged more as they wished.[57]

In August 1463, Nicodemo da Pontremoli, the Milanese ambassador resident in the Medici palace, wrote to his lord and master that "Cosimo and his supporters have no greater nor more ambitious enemy here than Dietisalvi." A year later, just a week after Cosimo's death, Dietisalvi himself wrote to Sforza that "Whereas while Cosimo was alive, decisions were left to him, now those who remain to govern the city are Piero, with the approval of several citizens who were brothers to Cosimo, and now have to be fathers to Piero, and must exercise great good will to maintain their friendship and to preserve the state."[58]

We may see from a letter that Cosimo wrote to Acciaiuoli, apparently in the early 1460s, that he was well aware how carefully he needed to tread with his old friends: "I have hesitated to write, expecting and wanting to have a letter first from you; not out of pride or any other desire to prevail over you . . . but to have some assurance of your good will toward me, such as I have toward you and your affairs." After a six-month silence from Acciaiuoli, Cosimo wrote again "to assure you that I bear toward you that same love and affection that I have always borne in the past . . . and that I am sure Piero and Giovanni will always bear." He urged Agnolo to return from Milan to Florence "for your own good and that of your children and for the good of our city, and the pleasure of your friends, and because it would give me the greatest happiness I could have in this world, since it seems to me that you understand how to take care of the republic of our city and know how it should be preserved in that good and peaceful state which it presently enjoys, and because my sons would regain another father in their every need."[59]

In fact, Piero proved to be much less inclined than his father to consult respectfully with old friends and to represent himself as only "first among equals."[60] He also lacked the innate "authority" that Cosimo's biographer, Vespasiano, saw as the key to the ruling group's acceptance of his leadership. With Cosimo gone, many prominent statesmen demanded a greater share of influence, increasingly represented as the triumph of republican liberty over a Medici tyranny. In September 1465, Dietisalvi Neroni reported to Sforza that "the people [of Florence] are very gratified to have regained their liberty." He attributed this to the fact that the Medici were obliged to rely more on their friends in government; "Piero and Luca Pitti now have more need of each other than in the past, and have more love and trust for one another than ever before."[61] Earlier the same year, Marco Parenti, who had married Alessandra Strozzi's daughter Caterina, had written to his Strozzi brothers-in-law that Piero de' Medici's "reputation" was "much diminished;" although "previously everyone was accustomed to going to him to consult on public affairs as well as private . . . Messer Luca Pitti [now] held court at his house, where a great part of the citizens went to consult on matters of government."[62]

In Florence, republican liberty meant partly the opportunity for a higher proportion of the ruling class to acquire a larger share of the patronage pie, consisting of access to offices of the state, from which men derived honor, profit, and influence. In these circumstances, it was impossible to entirely separate *res publica* (the affairs of the state), from which men derived a good part of their identity, from *res privata*, including friendship in its various senses. Some of the dissidents' grievances against the Medici stemmed from the family's failure, as their network of patronage expanded to embrace almost the entire city, to fulfill their obligations to their oldest and most important friends. After Piero had consistently failed to promote Agnolo Acciaiuoli's sons-in-law, Agnolo complained to Piero, observing that they had also been badly treated in the tax assessment, despite his own strenuous recommendation of their interests: "God give me patience; if you do not defend your friends and relatives you are not attending to your business."[63]

A very similar complaint was made by Filippo di Battista Arnolfi, son of another of Cosimo's oldest friends. His father, Battista di Doffo Arnolfi, had written to Cosimo in 1427, rejoicing in the results of a scrutiny for the state's highest offices, which admitted many new men from the ranks of the Medici partisans, despite the efforts of the entrenched regime to prevent this. "There is no end to the madness, or rather boldness of those who have governed us in the past. They are like horses without bridles. Now they have a tough bit in their mouths and will have to rein themselves in, or else their mouths will be broken."[64]

Forty years later, in 1466, Filippo used the very same simile to suggest to Piero that the Medici should now rein themselves in. Invoking his father's association with Piero's—"although I am not equal in virtue to my father as you are to yours"—he went on:

> Nevertheless, impelled by that fidelity that my Battista owned to your Cosimo I am emboldened to tell you for once what is in my heart, without worrying that your Magnificence may correct me . . . Piero, I have been wanting to tell you for many months now that you are sowing those seeds that Jason sowed on the island of Colchis.

Here he referred to Jason's quest for the Golden Fleece: the king of Colchis, an ancient city on the Black Sea, promised to give Jason the fleece if he could successfully perform three tasks, one of which was to sow the teeth of a dragon into a field and then defeat the warriors who sprouted from them.

> The two things that made your house great and can still do so if they are not entirely exhausted are the union of your friends, within, and without the city . . . There are four par-

ties of importance in the city, yours, and those of Luca Pitti, Dietisalvi Neroni, and the party of the middle (that of Agnolo Accaiuoli). Luca is about to join up with Dietisalvi, which will be the worst possible thing for you and for the city . . . You have a tough bit in your mouth, but the situation is not irremediable . . . If there is any issue between yourself and Luca Pitti, I advise you to settle it, making plain your union, so that you may be the head of the friendship of this city as Cosimo was in the past.[65]

This last phrase recalls both Aristotle's and Matteo Palmieri's descriptions of friendship as "the sole link that binds cities together."

In August 1466, impelled by a mixture of personal interest and patriotism, Acciaiuoli, Pitti, Dietisalvi Neroni, and Tommaso Soderini charged Piero with having betrayed the republic and the obligations he owed to his friends and challenged his leadership of the party. They were defeated, as Arnolfi's analysis had predicted, by a combination of loyalty from the Medici family's Florentine friends and the decisive intervention with armed support of their most faithful foreign friend, the Duke of Milan. Luca Pitti was reconciled to Piero with rewards in the form of offices and a marriage between his daughter and Giovanni Tornabuoni, a close Medici relative who later became manager of their bank.[66]

A final epistolary exchange between Piero de' Medici and Agnolo Acciaiuoli, after the conspiracy was crushed, reflects each man's perception that the other had broken faith with him.[67] Acciauoli, envisaging a balance sheet of obligations between their two houses accumulated over thirty years, saluted

Piero as his honored brother; invoking the exile he suffered for supporting Cosimo in 1433, he declared: "I laugh at what I see . . . God has put it in your power to cancel all the accounts I have with you, and you do not know how to do it. For your father's sake my *patria* and my position were taken from me; you are in a position to restore them."

Piero coolly parried Acciauoli's opening defiance: "Your laughter has prevented me from crying, although I was sorry for your ill fortune . . . You say you were exiled on my father's account, and for having saved what belonged to him. I do not deny your friendship with my father and with us, which ought to have made you regard me as a son, and as such I considered myself." Having noted the reciprocal obligations of friendship as honorary kinship, Piero proceeded to remind Acciaiuoli of the point Cicero made in *De Amicitia*: true friends cannot expect one another to act in a manner contrary to good faith or the good of the republic, because the virtues and obligations of friends and citizens cannot be distinguished. And, whereas Cosimo and his friends had been on the side of virtue thirty years earlier, in obeying the Signoria's edicts, while their enemies—in attempting to prevent the new Priors from recalling Cosimo—had set themselves against the republic, now Acciaiuoli's attempt to replace Piero as leader of the Medici party had led him to rebel against the state:

> Your guilt is manifest and so great that neither my intercession nor that of any other person would be of any avail. My nature is to forget and forgive you, and all who have shown

me enmity and hostility. I have pardoned every offense; the republic cannot and should not do so because it sets a bad example, as you know better than I, having had experience of such matters and having proclaimed it in public and in private . . . You were banished with my father and were recalled with him, according to the pleasure of the republic, which has full power over us . . . I do not conceive that our friendship was in any way hurtful or dishonorable to you, as can be clearly demonstrated, and if obligations and benefits were weighed, perhaps the scale would not be equal, although from what you write you do not seem to think so. I always considered myself obligated to you, but if you examine your conscience you will see that you have exempted me from any obligations; nevertheless I am willing to remain your debtor insofar as it touches me privately, but the public injury I cannot, will not and may not pardon.

There may have been some irony in his concluding vow: "For myself personally I forget everything, forgive all wrongs, and remain as a son ought to be toward such a father."

Largely as a consequence of getting caught in the cross fire between the Medici and the enemies of their political ambitions, the leaders of the wealthy and influential, but relatively apolitical, Strozzi lineage spent the central decades of the fifteenth century far from the political epicenter of their city, where friendships could so easily be consumed in political firefights. Outside the blazing inner circle of power, men like the merchant Marco Parenti, the son-in-law whom Alessandra Strozzi judged to have only "a very small share of influence in the state," might prove to be extraordinarily faithful friends, even under the most exigent conditions.[68] Parenti was remarkable for his tenacious defense of his Strozzi in-laws' interests and for his tireless efforts, reflected in his extensive correspondence with Alessandra, Filippo, and Lorenzo, to have them repatriated despite Medici intransigence; on one occasion, he even rousted Piero from his bed in the middle of the night to plead their cause. Parenti was also the trusted arbitrator of another great family marginalized by exile to the fringe of the Florentine political scene; he acted as "amicable" go-between and "chosen common friend" of Leon Battista Alberti and his kinsman Bernardo d'Antonio, when they came to divide the family palace in 1468.[69]

Parenti was also devoted to his wife, Caterina, and showered her with gifts. Alessandra's claim in a letter to her eldest son, Filippo, that "he's always saying to her, if you want anything ask me for it . . . he feels he can't do enough having things made" is borne out by the extensive list of the couple's possessions in the inventory of the house Marco lavishly furnished for his new bride.[70] After their marriage, Parenti became the mainstay of his mother-in-law and a close friend to Filippo and Lorenzo. A testimony to his affection for them was the care he gave to designing a silver belt buckle for Filippo. In a note that accompanied his gift, he described it as "a fantasy in my own style," incorporating a message in three parts. These were "you, to whom I am sending it . . . the place where I am sending it to you . . . I who am sending

it to you." It bore the Strozzi arms—a number of moons—
and a device of Parenti's own, which represented time, symbolized by a circle. There was also a salutary motto "that says
UTI FERT RES, which means, that's the way things go, to signify
that matters and actions are to be accommodated to the
times," perhaps a reference to the need for patience in their
joint endeavors to accomplish the Strozzi return to their native city.[71]

When the youngest of Alessandra's sons, Matteo, died at
the age of twenty-three in Naples, where he had recently
joined his brothers in the family business, Parenti wrote to
each of them expressing his grief in the warmest possible
terms of friendship and love. Seeming, indeed, to be that
"other self" that Cicero hoped to encounter in a friend,
Parenti, addressing Filippo as "most dear, like a brother to
me," told him:

> Since my father died I have not felt such pain, although two
> of my sons and two cousins by blood have died, which I
> thought had distressed me greatly enough; now that seems
> nothing by comparison with this . . . I think of your situa-
> tion and imagine that I am looking at you . . . and then there
> is your mother, whom I cannot remember without tears,
> considering what adversity she has suffered in such a brief
> time . . . Try to give her some support in her woes; no-one
> knows better than you how to do this, since you understand
> her heart so well . . . I had written thus far, and now a letter
> from you to Caterina has arrived. This renewed my grief,

and being so moved to tears myself, and thinking how she will feel, I haven't had the heart to give it to her yet . . . For the moment I feel so distressed that I'm incapable of writing any more . . .[72]

⌒

By the early sixteenth century, as foreign invaders erupted into the peninsula, the occasions of crisis and trial in which friendship might be tested extended far beyond the previous century's partisan upheavals. Men feared the loss, not only of fathers and friends, but of their very fatherland. As time-honored social structures began to crumble under the strain of inevitable change, Florentines drew sustenance, as they had in their discussions of friendship at the *certame coronario* almost a century earlier, from the time-tested consolations of classical and Christian wisdom.

Machiavelli, desperately seeking a solution to the problem of how to preserve his beloved *patria*, finding himself disappointed by patrons, unable to refrain from derogating the lowly companions of his exile, and always distrustful of women—whom he believed needed, like Fortune, to be conquered rather than loved—turned to those he considered his truest and most faithful friends, in whom he could always trust: the writers of classical Rome. Whereas Leon Battista Alberti, attempting to assess the quality of friendship, chose to rely on experience rather than learning, Machiavelli sought comfort in the company of his books. With a hint, despite his godless reputation, of the eucharistic (as John Najemy observed), he wrote to his friend Vettori:

> When evening comes, I return home, and go into my study, and at the threshold I take off my ordinary clothes, covered in mud and dirt, and I put on regal and courtly garments; and reclothed appropriately, I enter into the ancient courts of ancient men, where, lovingly received by them, I feed on that food which only is mine and for which I was born. And there I am not ashamed to speak to them, and to ask them the reasons for their actions; and they, in kindness, answer me; and for four hours I do not feel boredom, I forget every affliction, I do not fear poverty or tremble at death: I give myself over entirely to them.[73]

Michelangelo did not retreat from experience into learning to find friends; nor did he feel constrained to choose between the friendship of God and man. In his letters and his sonnets, friendship and love—erotic, intellectual and spiritual—for women and men, are fused in the language of Christian Neoplatonism, and of the Florentine vernacular (of Dante and Petrarch) within the framework of relationships that also involved patronage. The drawings he gave as gifts to his friends, like the sonnets he addressed to them, were full of profound personal feeling. To Tommaso Cavalieri, he sent a sensuous drawing of Ganymede ravished by a giant bird (see Figure 3.12), and in one of his many sonnets dedicated to Cavalieri, he wrote:

3.12. Michelangelo Buonarroti, attributed, *The Rape of Ganymede*. This drawing is probably very similar to the one Michelangelo presented to his friend Tommaso Cavalieri.

Happy that hour (O strongly I believe),
When in one moment time and day and sun
Will stop their ancient race with no alarms,
And I, not through my merit, shall receive
My gracious lord I sought, my only one,
Forever in my unworthy ready arms.[74]

Michelangelo and Vittoria Colonna, a Roman noblewoman and gifted humanist writer married to the Marchese
of Pescara, Ferrante d'Avolos, were passionate correspondents. The range of their emotional relationship is revealed
in the many sonnets he addressed to her, once asking of himself:

You make me soar so high, . . .
why then do I not fly
Much higher, having your swift wings, and reach
The beauty of your eyes,
And stay with you forever? Did not God
promise to give our bodies paradise?
Perhaps it is my luck that I should have
Body and soul asunder, through your grace,
And that my soul alone should reach your face.

Of the work that she commissioned from him, his drawing
of a *Pieta* was particularly dear to her heart.

Three years after Vittoria's death, Michelangelo wrote of
her to Giovan Francesco Fattucci: "Death has taken from me
a great friend *(amico)*." To use the masculine of the noun
"friend" was to pay Vittoria a tremendous compliment, since

women were considered by Renaissance men as imperfect and incapable of virtue and, therefore, of true friendship. Michelangelo went further, describing Vittoria in a sonnet as "a man in a woman, indeed a God." "For love of her," as he wrote, he made one of his most moving drawings, choosing to depict the still living, suffering, and so human Christ on his cross (Figure 3.13). For Michelangelo, as for the protagonists of the *certame coronario,* Christ remained, as he affirmed in one of his last sonnets, the only utterly reliable and true friend;

> that Love divine that, here,
> To take us, opened his arms on a cross and bled.[75]

3.13. Michelangelo Buonarroti, *Christ on the Cross*, presentation drawing for his friend Vittoria Colonna.

# Dramatis Personae: Some Leading Actors on the Florentine Scene

Acciaiuoli, Agnolo, patrician politician, and one of the major Medici friends who in 1466 led a conspiracy against them

Alberti, Leon Battista, patrician cleric, architect, and humanist writer; author of *On the Family*, Chapter four of which was entitled "On Friendship;" poet and organizer of the *certame coronario*, a competition held in the cathedral of Florence for the best poem on friendship

Altoviti, Bindo, Florentine banker and friend of Raphael and Michelangelo

Ammanattini, Manetto (The Fat Carpenter), butt of the practical joke recounted in the tale of *Il grasso legnaiuolo*, engineered by Brunelleschi and his friends

Angelico, Fra, friar at the Dominican convent of San Marco and painter of images of the saints for Cosimo de' Medici

Antoninus, Saint, prior of the convent of San Marco, later archbishop of Florence, and author of prescriptions for personal devotion

## Dramatis Personae

Apollonio di Giovanni, painter of decorated furniture and illuminated manuscripts

Aristotle, classical Greek author of treatises on *Ethics* and *Politics* discussing friendship

Augustine, Saint, late classical and early Christian writer, one of the four Fathers of the Church

Benci, Giovanni, writer and friend of Leonardo da Vinci, who painted his sister Ginevra's portrait

Bertoldo di Giovanni, sculptor and friend of Lorenzo; he lived in the Medici palace

Boccaccio, Giovanni, one of the "three crowns" of Florence, who along with Dante and Petrarch revived the classics and were models for vernacular literature

Botticelli, painter close to the circle of the young Lorenzo di Piero de' Medici

Bracciolini, Poggio, humanist friend of Cosimo de' Medici and chancellor of Florence

Brancacci, Branca, minor patrician and popular poet, exiled for his opposition to the Medici in 1434

Brancacci, Felice, member of exiled patrician family, former friend of Cosimo de' Medici, and patron of the Brancacci chapel frescoed by Masaccio and Masolino

Brunelleschi, Filippo, architect of the cathedral cupola and author of the trick played on the Fat Carpenter

Buonarroti, Michelangelo, sculptor and poet

Calderoni, Anselmo, popular poet and herald to the Signoria (governors of Florence)

Cavalieri, Tommaso, friend of Michelangelo and dedicatee of many of his sonnets

Cicero, ancient Roman statesman and author of *De Amicitia,* a treatise on friendship

Colonna, Vittoria, Roman noblewoman, humanist writer, and friend of Michelangelo

## Dramatis Personae

Dante Alighieri, author of *The Divine Comedy*, an encyclopedic poem relating the Christian and classical cultural traditions to the experience of the Florentine commune

Datini, Francesco, wealthy merchant of Prato and charitable patron

Della Stufa, Sigismondo, childhood crony of Lorenzo de' Medici, from a family of longtime Medici friends

Della Stufa, Ugo di Lorenzo, friend of the Medici family

Donatello, sculptor, friend of Brunelleschi and of Cosimo de' Medici

Donati, Lucrezia, Lorenzo de' Medici's ideal beloved

Ficino, Marsilio, Neoplatonic philosopher, friend and protégé of the Medici

Ghirlandaio, Domenico, painter of the frescoes for the Sassetti and Tornabuoni family chapels; in his workshop Michelangelo was trained

Giotto da Bondone, major Florentine artist of the early fourteenth century

Gozzoli, Benozzo, painter of frescoes at the convent of San Marco and in the Medici palace chapel

Leonardo da Vinci, painter

Lippi, Filippino, painter of a friendship portrait of himself and his patron, Piero del Pugliese

Lysippus, fifteenth century Roman maker of friendship medals

Machiavelli, Niccolò, best known for his political writings but author also of satirical plays and eloquent private letters

Martelli, Antonio di Ugolino, Medici friend and bank manager, and father-in-law of Michele del Giogante's son, Piero

Martelli, Braccio, childhood friend of Lorenzo de' Medici

Martelli, Domenico, father of Braccio

Martelli, Roberto, close Medici friend and manager of their bank; he oversaw Gozzoli's Medici chapel frescoes, in which his portrait appears

Masaccio, painter, friend of Brunelleschi and Donatello

Mazzei, Ser Lapo, Florentine notary

## Dramatis Personae

Medici, Averardo de', Cosimo's cousin and facilitator of the Medici party in the 1420s

Medici, Contessina de' Bardi de', wife of Cosimo de' Medici

Medici, Cosimo de', international banker, head of the largest and most powerful network of personal patronage in Florence, and major patron of art and culture

Medici, Giovanni de', younger son of Cosimo

Medici, Giuliano di Piero de', younger son of Piero di Cosimo, assassinated in 1478 in the Pazzi Conspiracy

Medici, Lorenzo di Piero de', elder son of Piero and grandson of Cosimo de' Medici

Medici, Lucrezia Tornabuoni de', wife of Piero di Cosimo de' Medici

Medici, Piero di Cosimo de', elder son of Cosimo, sponsor of the *certame coronario*

Michele del Giogante, accountant, entertainer, poet, and anthologist of Florentine popular culture; he was a Medici family friend and author of many reflections on friendship

Morelli, Giovanni, merchant and author of a memoir of advice to his heirs

Neri di Bicci, master of one of the busiest painter's workshops in Florence

Neroni, Dietisalvi, patrician politician, *aficionado* of Cicero's *De Amicitia*, and one of the intimate Medici friends who in 1466 led a conspiracy against them

Niccoli, Niccolò, humanist and friend of Cosimo

Niccolò Cieco, blind poet and friend of Michele del Giogante

Nori, Francesco, partner of the Medici bank in Florence

Palmieri, Matteo, merchant, statesman, and author of a treatise, *On Civic Life*

Paolo di Messer Pace da Certaldo, author of *Ricordi* and advice on social behavior

Parenti, Marco, merchant, patron of the arts, and friend of the exiled Strozzi family

## Dramatis Personae

Pazzi family, former friends of the Medici who conspired to assassinate Lorenzo and Giuliano in 1478

Pazzi, Andrea, friend and business associate of the Medici

Pazzi, Guglielmo, friend and brother-in-law of the young Lorenzo

Pelli, Ser Alesso, notary, prominent in charitable activities, and Medici household factotum

Petrarca, Francesco, author of Italian love poetry; he also revived interest in classical texts

Piovano Arlotto, antiauthoritarian priest and author of irreverent jokes and anecdotes

Pitti, Luca, longtime Medici friend and leader of the 1466 conspiracy again them; his portrait appears in the Medici palace chapel

Poliziano, Agnolo, poet and friend of Lorenzo and Giuliano de' Medici

Pugliese, Piero del, patron of Filippino Lippi with whom he is portrayed in a double friendship portrait

Rucellai, Giovanni, banker, author of a *zibaldone*, major patron of the arts, son-in-law of Palla Strozzi, and father-in-law to Lorenzo de' Medici's sister, Nannina

Sassetti, Bartolomeo, banker, Medici bookkeeper, and friend of Piovano Arlotto

Sassetti, Francesco, son of Bartolomeo, Medici friend and manager of their bank, portrayed in the Medici palace chapel frescoes, and patron of frescoes in Santa Trinita including Medici portraits

Sforza, Francesco, military captain, Duke of Milan after 1450, Cosimo de' Medici's closest foreign friend, and Florence's leading ally

Strozzi, Alessandra, widow of Marco Strozzi, exiled in 1434

Strozzi, Caterina, daughter of Alessandra and wife of Marco Parenti

Strozzi, Filippo, eldest son of Alessandra and Marco; after his father's exile, he set up business in Naples

Strozzi, Messer Palla di Nofri, wealthy and cultured banker, leader of his lineage, and rival of Cosimo de' Medici; he was exiled in 1434

Strozzi, Lorenzo, son of Alessandra

## Dramatis Personae

Temperani, Messer Manno, statesman, patron and friend of Apollonio di Giovanni

Tornabuoni, Giovanni, Medici friend, brother of Lucrezia (Piero de' Medici's wife), and manager of the Rome branch of the Medici bank; he is portrayed in the Medici chapel frescoes

Traversari, Ambrogio, humanist prior of Santa Maria degli Angeli and friend of Cosimo de' Medici and his younger brother, Lorenzo

Verrocchio, sculptor, painter, and master of the workshop in which Leonardo da Vinci was trained

Vespasiano da Bisticci, bookseller, biographer of Cosimo, gourmet, and godfather to Marco Parenti's son

Vespucci, Simonetta, Giuliano de' Medici's ideal beloved

# Notes

## Introduction

1. See Dale Kent, *The Rise of the Medici: Faction in Florence 1426–1434* (Oxford, 1978).

2. See *Cicero's Letters to Atticus*, ed. and trans. D. Shackleton Bailey (Cambridge, 1965–1968), 1, 18:1.

3. Saint Augustine, *Confessions*, trans. F. J. Sheed (Indianapolis, 2006), 4:4.

4. For a comprehensive survey of such definitions and the problems inherent in applying them to the remote past, see David Konstan, *Friendship in the Classical World* (Cambridge, 1997), introduction.

5. Marsilio Ficino, "Epistola ad Fratres Vulgaris" in *Supplementum Ficinianum*, ed. P. O. Kristeller (Florence, 1937), 1:113, cited by F. W. Kent, *Household and Lineage in Renaissance Florence: The Family Life of the Capponi, Ginori and Rucellai* (Princeton, 1977); see especially 46–47 on fathers and sons.

6. Dante Alighieri, *The Divine Comedy, Purgatorio,* 27; also *Inferno,* 15:83 on his literary patron and guide, Brunetto Latini. For this friendship pact, see below, 73.

7. Christopher Gill, "Peace of Mind and Being Yourself: Panaetius to Plutarch," in *Aufstieg und Niedergang der Römischen Welt,* ed. W. Haase and H. Temporini (Berlin, 1972–), pt. 2, vol. 36.7 (1994): 4599–4640, especially 4600, commenting upon Lionel Trilling, *Sincerity and Authenticity* (Cambridge, Mass., 1972).

8. On the role of ritual and performance in daily Florentine life, see Richard Trexler, *Public Life in Renaissance Florence* (New York, 1980). On the traditions and uses of rhetoric, see Ronald Witt, *"In the Footsteps of the Ancients": The Origins of Humanism from Lovato to Bruni* (Leiden, 2000).

9. See Erving Goffman, *The Presentation of Self in Everyday Life* (Garden City, N.J., 1959). Goffman's frame analysis has recently been applied to Renaissance Florence by the sociologist Paul McLean, *The Art of the Network: Strategic Interaction and Patronage in Renaissance Florence* (Durham, 2007).

10. Archivio di stato, Florence, Mediceo avanti il principato, II:147, Stefano di Francesco di Ser Segnia to Averardo de' Medici, 23 January 1429 (1430 modern style).

11. See particularly Ronald F. E. Weissman, "Taking Patronage Seriously: Mediterranean Values and Renaissance Society," in *Patronage, Art and Society in Renaissance Italy,* ed. F. W. Kent and Patricia Simons (Oxford, 1986), 25–45.

12. Felix Gilbert, "The Medici Megalopolis," Review of Richard Goldthwaite, *The Building of Renaissance Florence* (Baltimore, 1980), in *The New York Review of Books* (January 21, 1982): 62–66.

13. Leon Battista Alberti, *Opere volgari,* ed. Cecil Grayson (Bari, 1960–1973), 1:283; Luigi Graziano, *Clientelismo e sistema politico; Il caso dell'Italia* (Milan, 1980), 19–21.

14. Konstan, *Friendship,* 5.

15. Alan Silver, "Friendship and Trust as Moral Ideals: An Historical

Approach," *European Journal of Sociology* 30 (1990): 274–297, especially 275–276.

16. See Richard Goldthwaite, "The Medici Bank and the World of Florentine Capitalism," *Past and Present* 114 (1987): 3–31. On the relation of Renaissance banking to modern capitalism and values, see also Goldthwaite, "Urban Values and the Entrepreneur," in *L'impresa: industria commercio banca, secc XIII–XVIII,* ed. S. Cavaciocchi (Prato, 1991), 641–662. On Florentine commerce, business, and banking, see Goldthwaite, *The Economy of Renaissance Florence* (Baltimore, 2008).

17. See Gene Brucker, "*Fede* and *Fiducia:* The Problem of Trust in Italian History, 1300–1500," in Brucker, *Living on the Edge in Leonardo's Florence: Selected Essays* (Berkeley, 2005), 83–103; Ronald F. E. Weissman, *Ritual Brotherhood in Renaissance Florence* (New York, 1982), 22–26.

18. Morgan made this observation while on trial in 1912 for violating the U.S. antitrust laws; extracts from the trial transcripts appear in Jean Strouse, *Morgan: American Financier* (New York, 2000), 9–13. For Cosimo's maxim about trust and wealth, see Angelo Poliziano, *I detti Piacevoli,* ed. Mariano Fresta (Siena, 1985), 56. For the staff of the Medici bank, see Raymond de Roover, *The Rise and Decline of the Medici Bank* (Cambridge, Mass., 1963).

19. See Marcus Tullius Cicero, *Laelius De Amicitia* (English and Latin), in *On Old Age. On Friendship. On Divination.,* trans. W. A. Falconer (Cambridge, Mass., 1923), 103–211.

20. Lauro Martines, *Strong Words* (Baltimore, 2001), discusses these borrowings in chap. 2, "The Verbal Web of Patronage."

21. "Only connect," the epigraph of E. M. Forster's novel *Howard's End,* is the title of a collection of essays by John Shearman, *Only Connect . . . : Art and the Spectator in the Italian Renaissance* (Princeton, 1992). Irving Lavin also used the phrase as the epigraph of his *Past-Present; Essays on Historicism in Art from Donatello to Picasso* (Berkeley, 1993).

22. As in ancient Rome; compare P. A Brunt, *The Fall of the Roman Republic and Related Essays* (New York, 1988), 124.

23. For a fuller exposition of these associations, see Dale Kent, *Cosimo de' Medici and the Florentine Renaissance* (New Haven, 2000).

24. See, for example, Diana Robin, *Publishing Women: Salons, the Presses and the Counter-Reformation in Sixteenth-Century Italy* (Chicago, 2007).

25. Dante Alighieri, *The Divine Comedy, Inferno*. On the roots of civic strife, enmity, and mistrust in the early fourteenth century, see also Dante's contemporaries, the chroniclers Dino Compagni and Giovanni Villani; *Dino Compagni's Chronicle of Florence*, ed. Daniel D. Bornstein (Philadelphia, 1986); *Cronica di Giovanni Villani*, ed. I. Moutier and F. Dragomanni (Florence, 1844–1845; repr. Frankfurt, 1969).

## 1. What Did Friendship Mean?

1. On the significance of the *certame coronario* in Florentine cultural life and its promoters and patrons, see G. Gorni, "Storia del Certame Coronario," *Rinascimento*, ser. 2, 12 (1972): 135–181; also Dale Kent, *Cosimo de' Medici and the Florentine Renaissance* (New Haven, 2000), 28, 43, 80–83, 90, 138, 211, 359. The poems, both those presented in the cathedral and others that were later added to the canon of texts on friendship commonly copied into personal chapbooks, are published in *De vera amicitia: i testi del primo certame coronario*, ed. Lucia Bertolini (Modena, 1993). For Alberti's description of the cupola, see Leon Battista Alberti, *On Painting and On Sculpture*, ed. and trans. Cecil Grayson (New York, 1972), 33; for Alberti's comment on the *certame coronario*, see the *Protesta* he addressed to the humanist judges, who decided none of the performers was worthy of being pronounced the winner, Bertolini, *De vera amicitia*, 501–502.

2. Marcus Tullius Cicero, *Laelius De Amicitia* (English and Latin),

in *Old Age. On Friendship. On Divination.*, trans. W. A. Falconer (Cambridge, Mass., 1923), 103–211.

3. Bertolini, *De vera amicitia*, 366–373.

4. Ibid., 286–287.

5. Ibid., 268.

6. Ibid., 285, 290–291.

7. Alberti, *Protesta*, in Bertolini, *De vera amicitia*, 506.

8. On the *zibaldoni* and other anthologies in which friendship poems appear, see D. Kent, *Cosimo de' Medici*, chap. 6; for the full texts of these poems, see Antonio Lanza, *Lirici toscani del quattrocento*, 2 vols. (Rome, 1973–1975).

9. Dietisalvi di Nerone di Nigi Dietisalvi (Neroni), *Ricordi*, Archivio di stato, Florence (henceforth ASF), Manoscritti 85, fols. 98r–100r. On Florentine learned culture and the school curriculum, see Paul Grendler, *Schooling in Renaissance Italy* (Baltimore, 1989), especially 120–124, 212–217; Robert Black, "Education and the Emergence of a Literate Society," in *Italy in the Age of the Renaissance*, ed. John M. Najemy (Oxford, 2004), 18–36, 29.

10. The major study setting Alberti's works in the social and cultural context of his life is Luca Boschetto, *Leon Battista Alberti e Firenze: biografia, storia, letteratura* (Florence, 2000). A study in English also useful on these themes is Anthony Grafton, *Leon Battista Alberti: Master Builder of the Italian Renaissance* (New York, 2000), especially chap. 1. For Alberti's verse for the *certame coronario*, see Bertolini, *De vera amicitia*, 383–385. Cosimo de' Medici's reflections on envy are recorded by his biographer, Vespasiano da Bisticci, *Le vite*, ed. Aulo Greco (Florence, 1970–1976), 2:167–211, especially 209–210.

11. See Giovanni Morelli, *Ricordi*, ed. Vittore Branca (Florence, 1956); Paolo da Certaldo, *Libro di buoni costumi*, ed. A. Schiaffini (Florence, 1945).

12. Alberti, *On Painting*, 33. See also on Alberti's friendship with Donatello, Gabriele Morolli, "Donatello e Alberti, 'amicissimi',"

in *Donatello-Studien, Italienische Forschungen, Kunsthistorisches Institut in Florenze Band XVI* (Munich, 1989), 43–67.

13. Leon Battista Alberti, *Opere volgari,* ed. Cecil Grayson (Bari, 1960–1973), 1:268.

14. See Aristotle, *Nicomachean Ethics,* trans. H. Rackham (Cambridge, Mass., 1926), bks. 8, 9.

15. For the Aristotelian basis of the ethics and politics of the early Italian communes, see Nicolai Rubinstein, "The Beginnings of Political Thought in Florence," *Journal of the Warburg and Courtauld Institutes* 5 (1942): 198–227.

16. See Matteo Palmieri, *Vita Civile,* ed. Gino Bellon (Florence, 1982); the treatise was written in 1439. See also *Giovanni Rucellai ed il suo Zibaldone,* ed. A. Perosa (London, 1960), 91–92; Agnolo Acciaiuoli, ASF, Carte Strozziane (henceforth CS) ser. 3, 27, c. 126.

17. Palmieri, *Vita Civile,* 4:161–163.

18. Bertolini, *De vera amicitia,* 198.

19. See particularly David Konstan, *Friendship in the Classical World* (Cambridge, 1991), especially chap. 4. A treatise attributed to Cicero's brother discussed friendship as a strategy to attract voters. Italian scholars of Italy's native tradition of political and personal patronage stretching back from the present through the Renaissance to classical Rome distinguish it from cultural or charitable patronage as "clientelismo;" see particularly Luigi Graziano, *Clientelismo e sistema politico: Il caso dell'Italia* (Milan, 1980).

20. See Peter Brown, *The Cult of the Saints: Its Rise and Function in Latin Christianity* (Chicago, 1981). Following Brown, the association of these ideas in Renaissance Florence is articulated at length in D. Kent, *Cosimo de' Medici,* chap. 9, and in Dale Kent, "Charity and Power in Renaissance Florence: Surmounting Cynicism in Historiography," *Common Knowledge* 9 (2003): 254–272.

21. Paolo da Certaldo, *Libro di buoni costumi,* 47, 73–74, discussed by

Ronald F. E. Weissman, *Ritual Brotherhood in Renaissance Florence* (New York, 1982), 41.

22. Alberti, *On Painting*, 74.

23. The account of this transaction is by Feo Belcari, popular poet, canon of the cathedral, and a close friend of the Medici. It is published by Howard Saalman, *Filippo Brunelleschi: The Cupola of Santa Maria del Fiore* (London, 1980), 276.

24. See Lanza, *Lirici toscani*, 1:240.

25. For the letter to Cosimo, ASF, Mediceo avanti il principato (henceforth, MAP), XIII, 27; that of Forese Sacchetti's friend is cited by F. W. Kent in "Lorenzo, amico degli uomini da bene: Lorenzo de' Medici and oligarchy," in *Lorenze il Magnifico e il suo mondo: Convegno internazionale di studi, Firenze*, (1992), 9–13, ed. Gian Carlo Garfagnini (Florence, 1994), 43–60, 57. On the language of the Medici letters, see Dale Kent, *The Rise of the Medici: Faction in Florence* (Oxford, 1978), especially introduction and pt. 1, chap. 1; for an attempt, not entirely successful, at a systematic sociological analysis of the language of friendship in Renaissance Florence, see Paul McLean, "A Frame Analysis of Favor Seeking in the Renaissance: Agency, Networks and Political Culture," *American Journal of Sociology* 104 (1998): 51–91; see also *The Art of the Network: Strategic Interaction and Patronage in Renaissance Florence* (Durham, 2007).

26. MAP, XII, 183; Benedetto Dei cited by F. W. Kent in "Lorenzo amico," 56.

27. Attention was first drawn to this work by Millard Meiss, "An Early Altarpiece from the Cathedral of Florence," *Metropolitan Museum of Art Bulletin*, ns. 12 (1954): 302–317. For more recent comment and bibliography, see Timothy Verdon, "The Intercession of Christ and the Virgin from Florence Cathedral: Iconographic and Ecclesiological Significance," in *Atti del VII centenario del Duomo*, 2; *La Cattedrale come spazio sacro*, ed. Timothy Verdon and Annalisa Innocenti (Florence, 2001), 130–149.

28. *Opera a ben vivere di Santo Antonino,* ed. Francesco Palermo (Florence, 1858), pt. 3, 149.

29. These works are discussed at length in D. Kent, *Cosimo de' Medici,* chap. 9.

30. For Tornabuoni's poem and the story of Tobias, see Lucrezia Tornabuoni de' Medici, *Sacred Narratives,* ed. and trans. Jane Tylus (Chicago, 2001), especially 48–49, 72–117. On the Bigallo, see Hanna Kiel, ed., *Il Museo del Bigallo a Firenze* (Milan, 1977); Howard Saalman, *The Bigallo: The Oratory and Residence of the Compagnia del Bigallo e della Misericordia in Florence* (New York, 1969).

31. See E. H. Gombrich, "Tobias and the Angel," in Gombrich, *Symbolic Images* (London, 1972), 26–30. Many Florentine representations of this theme are reproduced in Gertrude M. Achenbach, "The Iconography of Tobias and the Angel in Florentine Paintings of the Renaissance," *Marsyas* 3 (1943–1945): 71–86.

32. David Alan Brown, *Leonardo da Vinci: Origins of a Genius* (New Haven, 1998), chap. 2.

33. Dante Alighieri, *The Divine Comedy, Paradiso,* 4:46–48.

34. The panel by a follower of Baldovinetti is reproduced in Gombrich, "Tobias and the Angel." Botticini, himself, was a member of the company of the Archangel Raphael, known as *il Raffa,* which met in the church of Santo Spirito. He made several representations of Tobias and the archangels. See Lina Venturini, *Francesco Botticini* (Florence, 1994), for the altarpiece of the confraternity chapel in Santo Spirito, catalog no. 23, fig. 26; for the Doni altarpiece, catalog no. 61, 121–22 and 228, fig. 96, and also Alessandro Cecchi, "Agnolo e Maddalena Doni Committenti di Raffaello," in *Studi su Raffaello, atti del congresso internazione di studi* (Urbino-Firenze, 1984), ed. Micaela Sambucco Hamoud and Maria Letizia Strocchi (Urbino, 1987), 429–439.

35. See Lauro Martines, *Strong Words: Writing and Social Strain in the Italian Renaissance* (Baltimore, 2001), especially 16. A particularly bitter and virulent series of poems by Giovan Matteo di Meglio,

*Rime,* ed. Giuseppe Brincat (Florence, 1977) is directed not against patrons but failed friendship; they were originally inscribed in an anthology that Giovan Matteo compiled with his friend Michele del Giogante, Biblioteca Riccardiana, Florence, MS Riccardiana 2734. For Michele's extensive reflections on friendship, see below, chap. 2.

36. MAP IV, 79, Niccolò Carducci to Averardo de' Medici, 24 August 1431; ibid., III, 126, Bartolomeo de' Medici to Averardo de' Medici, 14 May 1431. See also ibid., V, 498, Niccolò Bonvanni to Averardo de' Medici, 17 February 1444.

37. Ibid., XXVIII, 1440, 21 August 1472; V, 568, 1 April 1445; V, 498, 1445.

38. McLean, *Art of the Network,* 35. For a particularly strong and sustained articulation of the anthropological view that in traditional societies, form constructs feeling, see Richard Trexler, *Public Life in Renaissance Florence* (New York, 1980), especially 132; also 133–158.

39. For a general analysis of Cosimo de' Medici's correspondents, see Anthony Molho, "Cosimo de' Medici: *Pater Patriae* or *padrino*?", *Stanford Italian Review* 1 (1979): 5–33.

40. MAP, V, 338, 2 August 1438; ibid., VII, 101, 29 May (no year given).

41. See Dale Kent, "I Medici in esilio: una vittoria di famiglia ed una disfatta personale," *Archivio storico italiano* CXXXII (1974): 3–63.

42. MAP, XVI, 15, 15 January 1441 (1442 modern style).

43. Matthew 26: 40. For Cosimo's letter, see CS ser. 3, 120, c. 138, 4 December 1436; see also CS ser. 3, 150, c. 108b, 31 May 1445: "Consider him as if you were doing this for me myself, because he is my very great friend."

44. MAP, VII, 89, June 1442; ibid., V, 485.

45. Ibid., VII, 90; XX, 116.

46. For a masterful account of the multiple resonances of early modern gift giving, balancing friendship with control, and generosity

with reciprocity, see Natalie Zemon Davis, *The Gift in Sixteenth-Century France* (Madison, WI, 2000).

47. MAP XX, 151.

48. Ibid., XI, 508, 53.

49. Ibid., V, 475; XI, 350.

50. MAP XVI, 27, 7 May 1445.

51. See Cicero, *De Amicitia*, bks. 11–12. For Acciaiuoli's view that the Medici party's actions were opposed to republican ideals, see Nicolai Rubinstein, *The Government of Florence under the Medici 1434–1494*, 2nd ed. (Oxford, 1997), pt. 2, and below, chap. 3.

52. Matthew 12: 30; MAP, XVI, 59; also II, 234; V, 337; Rucellai, *Zibaldone*, 9.

53. For a brilliant, but perhaps not sufficiently socially grounded, interpretation of this letter, see Luca Boschetto, "Incrociare le fonti: archivi e letteratura. Rileggendo la lettera di Leon Battista Alberti a Giovanni di Cosimo de' Medici, 10 aprile [1456?]," in *Medioevo e Rinascimento, Annuario del Dipartimento di Studi sul Medioevo e il Rinascimento dell'Universita di Firenze* XVII, n.s. XIV (2003): 243–264.

54. Ser Lapo Mazzei, *Lettere di un notaro a un mercante del secolo XIV: con altre lettere e documenti*, ed. Cesare Guasti (Florence, 1880), 1:191. The classic study of this friendship is by Iris Origo, *The Merchant of Prato: Francesco di Marco Datini 1335–1410* (New York, 1963). Their relationship was radically reinterpreted by Trexler, *Public Life*, chap. 5, in the light of his sociologically inspired thesis that even personal friendships were essentially public and social acts.

55. See Cicero's *Letters to Atticus*, ed. and trans. D. Shackleton Bailey (Cambridge, 1965–1968), 1, 18:1. For Cicero's other criteria of true friendship, see *De Amicitia*, 4:14–20, and for Mazzei's reference to these, *Lettere*, 1:83, 370.

56. Ibid., 1:3–5.

57. Ibid., 1:6, 2:179. For Michele's comment on charity, see Bertolini, *De vera amicitia*, 447–448.

58. The Ceppo Nuovo in 1452–1453 commissioned Fra Filippo to manage construction of a tabernacle over a well in the courtyard of their palace and to paint for it a *Madonna and Child*, with Datini and four Buonomini. See Jeffrey Ruda, *Fra Filippo Lippi* (London, 1993), 47.

59. Mazzei, *Lettere*, 2:56–58. For rather different interpretations of this incident, see Dale Kent, "Illegitimate and Legitimating Passions in Fifteenth-Century Florentine Political Discourses," *Cultural and Social History* 2, 2005: 1–14; Trexler, *Public Life*, chap. 5.

60. Mazzei, *Lettere*, 1:231, 325–328; 2:25–26.

61. Ibid., 1:7, 190, 340; 2:107.

62. MAP, V, 412, Bartolommeo Sassetti to Giovanni de' Medici; Mazzei, *Lettere*, 1:226–227; 2:25; see also Allen Grieco, "Alimentation et classes sociales à la fin du Moyen Âge et à la Renaissance," in *Histoire de l'alimentation*, ed. Jean-Louis Flandrin et Massimo Mantanari (Paris, 1996), 479–490.

63. Mazzei, *Lettere*, 1:32, 35.

64. Datini Archives, Prato, file 1080, Margherita Datini to Ser Lapo Mazzei, 10 April 1394, cited by Origo in *Merchant of Prato*, 211.

65. Mazzei, *Lettere*, 2:261–262, August 1410, Ser Lapo Mazzei to Cristofano di Bartolo, Datini's factor in Barcelona.

66. Alberti, *On Painting*, 79; Dante, *Purgatorio*, 8:3–5.

67. Cited by F. W. Kent, ed., *Bartolomeo Cederni and His Friends: Letters to an Obscure Florentine* (Florence, 1991), 12.

68. See Carlo Pedretti, "Leonardo, 1505 e dopo," in *La mente di Leonardo*, ed. Carlo Pedretti (Florence, 2006), 23.

69. "Un contratto di fratellanza," *Miscellanea storica senese* 4 (1896): 78–80. I owe this reference to Luke Syson.

70. Louis A. Waldman, "The Modern Lysippus: A Roman Quattrocento Medalist in Context," in *Perspectives on the Renaissance Medal, 1450–1650*, ed. Stephen K. Scher (New York, 2000), 97–113, 99.

71. On the Titian, see David Alan Brown and Sylvia Ferino Pagden, *Bellini, Giorgione, Titian and the Renaissance of Venetian Painting* (New

Haven, 2006), 264–267. For the Pontormo portrait and its inscription, see Carl Brandon Strehlke, et. al., *Pontormo, Bronzino and the Medici: The Transformation of the Renaissance Portrait in Florence* (Philadelphia, 2004), 64–66; the passage written on the paper is Cicero, *De Amicitia*, 6:22.

72. See Ronald Lightbown, *Mantegna* (Oxford, 1986), 459–460.

73. This portrait is further discussed below, 144.

74. For Antonio della Casa's request, see *Il Duomo di Firenze; Documentri sulla decorazione della Chiesa e del campanile tratti dall'archivio dell'opera per cura di Giovanni Poggi*, ed. Margaret Haines (Florence, 1988), 2:138–139.

75. On Medici friends' adoption of Medicean visual themes, see Dale Kent, "The Patronage of Cosimo de' Medici and His Friends in Relation to Desiderio da Settignano and His Circle," in *Atti del convegno su Desiderio da Settignano al Kunsthistoriches Institut* (Florence, 2007), ed. Louis Waldman and Fabio Vitucci (Florence, 2008); also D. Kent, *Cosimo de' Medici*. On the Dalla Lama commission, see Rab Hatfield, *Botticelli's Uffizi 'Adoration'* (Princeton, 1976).

76. On these portraits, see *The Chapel of the Magi: Benozzo Gozzoli's Frescoes in the Palazzo Medici-Riccardi, Florence*, ed. Christina Acidini Luchinat (London, 1994), "Medici and Citizens."

77. For these chapels, see Jean Cadogan, *Domenico Ghirlandaio, Artist and Artisan* (New Haven, 2000). The inventory of Sassetti's library in 1462, ASF, CS, ser. 2, 20, includes several works of Cicero, including *On Friendship*; see Albinia de la Mare, "The Library of Francesco Sassetti (1421–90)," in *Cultural Aspects of the Italian Renaissance: Essays in Honour of Paul Oskar Kristeller*, ed. Cecil H. Clough (Manchester, 1976), 160–201.

## 2. Where Did Friends Meet?

1. The decree can be found in Archivio di stato, Florence (henceforth ASF), Otto di Guardia 67, fol. 67v; it is cited as evidence

of the myriad collective activities in Renaissance Florence by
F. W. Kent, "'Un paradiso habitato da diavoli:' Ties of Loyalty
and Patronage in the Society of Medicean Florence," in *Le Radici
Cristiane di Firenze*, ed. Anna Benvenuti, Franco Cardini, and
Elena Giannarelli (Florence, 1994): 183–210, 184. On the crowds
that gathered at building sites, "so that it was very difficult to
pass along the street," see Luca Landucci, *Diario Fiorentino dal
1450 al 1516 di Luca Landucci, continuato da un anonimo fino al 1542*
(Florence, 1883), 57–58.

2. Above, 27–28, 31.

3. On the history and functions of the Piazza della Signoria, see
Nicolai Rubinstein, *The Palazzo Vecchio, 1298–1532: Government, Ar-
chitecture and Imagery in the Civic Palace of the Florentine Republic* (New
York, 1995), chap. 3; for a very different view of the significance
of this space, see Marvin Trachtenberg, *Dominion of the Eye: Ur-
banism, Art and Power in Early Modern Florence* (Cambridge, 1997),
pts. 1 and 3.

4. Saint Augustine, *Confessions*, trans. F. J. Sheed (Indianapolis, 2006),
4:4. For the influence of Augustine on Renaissance thought, see
Carol E. Quillen, *Rereading the Renaissance: Petrarch, Augustine, and
the Language of Humanism* (Ann Arbor, Michigan, 1998); William J.
Bouwsma, "The Two Faces of Humanism: Stoicism and Augus-
tinianism in Renaissance Thought," in Bouwsma, *A Usable Past:
Essays in European Cultural History* (Berkeley, 1990), 19–73. David
Konstan, *Friendship in the Classical World* (Cambridge, 1997) is the
essential study in English of attitudes to friendship in the classical and early Christian period whose cultural traditions strongly
shaped the ideas and behavior of Renaissance Florentines.

5. *De vera amicitia: i testi del primo certame coronario*, ed. Lucia Bertolini
(Modena, 1993), 288.

6. For the scene with Buto, see Leon Battista Alberti, *Opere volgari*,
ed. Cecil Grayson (Bari, 1960–1973), 1:263–265.

7. See Antonio Lanza, *Polemiche e Berte letterarie nella Firenze del primo
Rinascimento (1375–1449)*, 2nd ed. (Rome, 1989), 374.

8. For an account of cross-class relationships that focuses more on weighing their positive and negative aspects, see F. W. Kent, "'Be Rather Loved than Feared': Class Relations in Quattrocento Florence," in *Society and Individual in Renaissance Florence*, ed. William J. Connell (Berkeley, 2002): 1–43.

9. On popular culture and charity at San Martino, see Dale Kent, *Cosimo de' Medici and the Florentine Renaissance* (New Haven, 2000), 43–54; Dale Kent, "The *Buonomini di San Martino:* 'Charity for the Glory of God, the Honour of the City, and the Commemoration of Myself,'" in *Cosimo 'il Vecchio' de' Medici, 1389–1464,* ed. Francis Ames Lewis (Oxford, 1992), 49–67.

10. On Michele del Giogante's house and its neighborhood, see Dale Kent, 'The Lodging-House of All Memories': An Accountant's Home in Renaissance Florence," *The Journal of the Society of Architectural Historians* 66 (2007): 444–463; see also Michele's tax reports, especially that of 1427; ASF, Catasto 50, 515r–516v, new numeration.

11. ASF, Mediceo avanti il principato (henceforth MAP), XXIII, 709. On this incident, see Dale V. and F. W. Kent, "Two Vignettes of Florentine Society in the Fifteenth Century," *Rinascimento* XXIII (1983): 237–260, especially 253–260, "Lorenzo de' Medici and the Lads from the Canto alla Macina." For the fantasy kingdom located in this Medici neighborhood, see Rab Hatfield, *Journal of the Warburg and Courtauld Institutes* 33 (1970): 107–161; on the festive and ritual life of Florence, see Richard Trexler, *Public Life in Renaissance Florence* (New York, 1980).

12. Dale Kent, "Michele del Giogante's House of Memory," in *Society and the Individual:* 110–136. The treatise is in the Biblioteca Riccardiana, Florence (henceforth Riccardiana), MS Riccardiana 2734, fols. 28r–29v.

13. Ibid., fol. 28r.

14. Cited by Yvonne Elet in "Seats of Power: The Outdoor Benches of Early Modern Florence," *Journal of the Society of Architectural*

*Historians* 61 (2002): 444–469. On this subject, see also F. W. Kent, "Palaces, Politics and Society in Fifteenth-Century Florence," *I Tatti Studies* 2 (1987): 41–72.

15. Marcus Tullius Cicero, *Laelius De Amicitia* (English and Latin), in *Old Age. On Friendship. On Divination.*, trans. W. A. Falconer (Cambridge, Mass., 1923), 103–211, 4:14–16, 125.

16. D. Kent, *Cosimo de' Medici*, 53. On the anthology of material relating to Sforza that Michele del Giogante made for Piero de' Medici, see Dale Kent, "Florentine Renaissance Chapbooks: Re-Presenting Current Events to Conform to Christian, Classical, and Civic Ideals," in *Religious Rituals, Images and Words. The Varieties of Cultural Expression in Late Medieval and Early Modern Europe*, ed. F. W. Kent and Charles Zika (Turnhout, 2005), 277–295.

17. Letter of Michele del Giogante to Piero de' Medici, 24 May 1454, MAP, XVII, 108.

18. On the Martelli marriage alliance and Michele's neighbors and business associates, see D. Kent, "The Lodging-House of All Memories," 447–450, 460, n40.

19. Bertolini, *De vera amicitia*, 446.

20. Riccardiana, MSS 2729, 2734, 2735. The sonnets by Giovan Matteo Meglio on the theme of failed friendships are published in Giuseppe Brincat, ed. *Giovan Matteo di Meglio* (Florence, 1977).

21. See Cicero, *De Amicitia*, 18:65.

22. Antonio Lanza, *Lirici toscani del quattrocento* (Rome, 1973–1975), 1:671–672.

23. Ibid., 680–681.

24. Francesco Flamini, *La lirica Toscana del Rinascimento anteriore ai tempi del Magnifico* (Pisa, 1891), 287.

25. Riccardiana, MS 2735, fol. 171r. Michele designated place 59 of his memory treatise as the chessboard hung above the chest near his bed (Riccardiana MS 2734, fol. 29r). Cosimo's biographer, Vespasiano da Bisticci, *Le vite*, ed. Aulo Greco (Florence, 1970–

1976), 2:195, refers to the chess matches between the statesman and the renowned Magnolino.

26. Lanza, *Lirici toscani*, 1:671; for the poem commissioned by the Medici men, ibid., 667–668.

27. MAP, XII, 207, Michele del Giogante to Cosimo de' Medici, 18 January 1449 (1450 modern style). For the letter to Carlo di Palla Strozzi, see Flamini, *La lirica toscana*, 598.

28. MAP, V, 348, 25 December 1438.

29. On the role of great palaces in social and political life, see F. W. Kent, "Palaces, Politics and Society," 45; Brenda Preyer, "Planning for Visitors at Florentine Palaces," *Renaissance Studies* 12 (1998): 357–374.

30. See MAP, V, 284, 297, 298, and VIII, 413; this last letter of Pigello to Giovanni, written on 9 March 1461, urged him to come to see the splendid new building the duke of Milan had given them to house the bank. On the Portinari family's commercial and personal ties to the Medici, see D. Kent, *Cosimo de' Medici*, 356–357, and Raymond de Roover, *The Rise and Decline of the Medici Bank* (Cambridge, Mass., 1963), 262, 387.

31. On Alesso, see Dale Kent, "A Window on Cosimo de' Medici, *Paterfamilias* and Politician, from Within His Own Household: The Letters of His Personal Assistant, Ser Alesso Pelli," in *Florence and Beyond: Culture, Society and Politics in Renaissance Italy*, ed. David S. Peterson with Daniel E. Bornstein (Toronto, 2008), 353–365.

32. MAP, XVI, 101. For the full range of Alesso's activities, see Kent, *Cosimo de' Medici*, passim.

33. See successively, MAP, V, 374, 396, 340.

34. See successively, MAP, V, 374, 301, 466; also ASF, Catasto, 62, fol. 277r.

35. Ibid., XI, 268; V, 305, 451.

36. Ibid. V, 591, 596, 597, 605.

37. Ibid., V, 509; VII, 253.
38. Ibid., V, 238; VI, 574. On the Canal Officials and Lorenzo's assumption of this office, see F. W. Kent, *Lorenzo de' Medici and the Art of Magnificence* (Baltimore, 2004), 24.
39. MAP, VI, 545.
40. Ibid.; Cicero, *De Amicitia*, 4:14–16, 125.
41. Giovanni Rucellai, *Giovanni Rucellai ed il suo Zibaldone*, ed. Alessandro Perosa (London, 1960), 102.
42. On this community, see Nicholas Eckstein, *The District of the Green Dragon: Neighborhood Life and Social Change in Renaissance Florence* (Florence, 1995).
43. See Nerida Newbigin, *Feste d'Oltrarno: Plays in Churches in Fifteenth-Century Florence* (Florence, 1996); *The Brancacci Chapel: Form, Function and Setting*, ed. Nicholas Eckstein, (Florence, 2007); Augustine, *Confessions*, trans. F. L. Sheed (Indianapolis, 2006), 4:10–11.
44. Ronald F. E. Weissman, "Brothers and Strangers: Confraternal Charity in Renaissance Florence," *Historical Reflections / Reflections historiques* 15 (1988): 27–45, 27. On confraternities, see particularly Ronald F. E. Weissman, *Ritual Brotherhood in Renaissance Florence* (New York, 1982) and John Henderson, *Piety and Charity in Late Medieval Florence* (Oxford, 1994).
45. See Judith Brown, *Immodest Acts: The Life of a Lesbian Nun in Renaissance Italy* (New York, 1986), especially 117–131.
46. See the manuscripts of personal anthologies in Biblioteca Nazionale, Florence (henceforth BNF), II:VII:4, fol. 4v; also Magliabechiana VII, 375, fols. 16v, 18r.
47. Michael Rocke, *Forbidden Friendships: Homosexuality and Male Culture in Renaissance Florence* (New York, 1996), 149.
48. Ibid., 149.
49. See Henderson, *Piety and Charity*, 436–437.
50. See *Ricordanze di Bartolomeo Masi calderaio fiorentino dal 1478 al 1526*, ed. O Corazzini (Florence, 1906), especially 78–81, 256–257.

51. Giovanni Morelli, *Ricordi*, ed. Vittore Branca (Florence, 1956), 253–254, 260; Paolo di Ser Pace da Certaldo, *Libro di buoni costumi*, ed. A. Schiaffini (Florence, 1945), 215–217.

52. Cited by F. W. Kent in "Palaces, Politics and Society," 60. On confraternal prohibitions, see Weissman, *Ritual Brotherhood*, 88.

53. See William J. Connell and Giles Constable, *Sacrilege and Redemption in Renaissance Florence: The Case of Antonio Rinaldeschi* (London, 1998).

54. See Piovano Arlotto, *Motti e Facezie*, ed. Gianfranco Folena (Milan, 1953); also the study by F. W. Kent and Amanda Lillie, "The Piovano Arlotto: New Documents," in *Florence and Italy: Renaissance Studies in Honour of Nicolai Rubinstein*, ed. Peter Denley and Caroline Elam (London, 1988, 347–367). The authors publish a photograph of the inn and identify and describe many of the historical characters of the *Motti e Facezie;* see especially 348.

55. Arlotto, *Motti e Facezie*, 85.

56. Cited by F. W. Kent in "Un paradiso habitato da diavoli," 186. For the detailed account kept of food consumed by the *mensa* of the Signoria, see Allen J. Grieco, "From the Cookbook to the Table: A Florentine Table and Italian Recipes of the Fourteenth and Fifteenth Centuries," in *Du manuscrit à la table: essais sur la cuisine au Moyen Âge et répertoires des manuscrits médiévaux contenant des recettes culinaire*, ed. Carole Lambert (Montreal, 1992), 29–38.

57. See F. W. Kent, *Bartolommeo Cederni and His Friends: Letters to an Obscure Florentine* (Florence, 1991), 104–105. On Vespasiano's love of eating, see M. Cagni, *Vespasiano e il suo epistolario* (Rome, 1969), 41.

58. See below, 192, 210. On the surprisingly neglected, although fascinating, figure of Palla Strozzi, see Vespasiano, *Le vite*, 2:139–165; on his largely apolitical stance, see Heather Gregory, "Palla Strozzi's Patronage and Pre-Medicean Florence," in *Patronage, Art and Society in Renaissance Italy*, ed. F. W. Kent and Patricia Simons (Oxford, 1987), 201–220.

59. Cagni, *Vespasiano e il suo epistolario,* 123. Compare this passage with Cicero, *De Amicitia,* 19:69–70, 179.

60. See Giovanni Boccaccio, *The Decameron,* trans. Mark Musa and Peter Bondanella (New York, 1982), 419–425, fifth day, eighth story. On Botticelli's panel, see *Botticelli and Filippino: L'inquietudine e la grazia nella pittura fiorentina del Quattrocento,* ed. Daniel Arasse, Pierluigi De Vecchi, and Jonathan Katz Nelson (Milan, 2004), especially 102–104.

61. For this extraordinary story, which overturns the traditional assumption that the Medici themselves were the patrons of the Uccello panels described in the 1492 inventory of their palace, see Francesco Caglioti, *Donatello e i Medici. Saggio di storia dell'arte sul David e la Giuditta* (Florence, 2000), chap. 6.

62. Ser Lapo Mazzei, *Lettere di un notaro a un mercante del secolo XIV: con altre lettere e documenti,* ed. Cesare Guasti (Florence, 1880), 2:33. Compare the discussion of their friendship above, chap. 1, and especially on Ser Lapo's strong sense of the social significance of food, see Grieco, "From the Cookbook to the Table," 37.

63. See Antonio Manetti, *Vita di Filippo Brunelleschi: preceduta da la novella del Grasso,* ed. Domenico de' Robertis, with introduction and notes by Giuliano Tanturli (Milan, 1976). For the interpretation of this tale, especially in terms of cross-class friendships, see particularly Lauro Martines, *An Italian Renaissance Sextet: Six Tales in Historical Context* (New York, 1994); also Guido Ruggiero, "Mean Streets, Familiar Streets, or The Fat Woodcarver and the Masculine Spaces of Renaissance Florence," in Roger Crum and John T. Paoletti, eds., *Renaissance Florence: A Social History* (New York, 2006), 295–310. On Brunelleschi's circle of artistic and literary friends, see Giuliano Tanturli, "Rapporti del Brunelleschi con gli ambienti letterari fiorentini," in *Filippo Brunelleschi, la sua opera e il suo tempo* (Florence, 1980), 1:125–144.

64. On the cooperation among Medici patrons and artists in decorating San Lorenzo, see Dale Kent, "The Patronage of Cosimo

de' Medici and His Friends in Relation to Desiderio da Settignano and His Circle, in *Atti del convegno su Desiderio da Settignano
al Kunsthistoriches Institut"* (Florence, 2007), ed. Louis Waldman
and Fabio Vitucci (Florence, 2008). For the friendship between Alberti and Donatello, see Gabriele Morolli, "Donatello e
Alberti, 'amicissimi': Suggestioni e suggerimenti albertiani nelle
immagini architettoniche dei rilievi donatelliani," in *Donatello-
Studien, Italienische Forschungen Kunsthistorisches Institut in Florenz*
XVI (1989): 43–67.

65. For the cooperation between Desiderio and Neri di Bicci, see
Neri di Bicci, *Le Ricordanze*, ed. Bruno Santi (Pisa, 1976). On Mi-
chelangelo's workshop, see William E. Wallace, *Michelangelo at San
Lorenzo: The Genius as Entrepreneur* (Cambridge, 1994), 101–102.

66. Rocke, *Forbidden Friendships*, 149.

67. Manetti, *Vita*, 31.

68. F. W. Kent, "Lorenzo di Credi, His Patron Iacopo Bongianni and
Savonarola," *The Burlington Magazine* 125 (1983): 539–541.

69. See Michelle O'Malley, "Contracts, Designs and the Exchange of
Ideas Between Patrons and Clients in Renaissance Italy," in *Artistic
Exchange and Cultural Translation in the Italian Renaissance*, ed. Stephen J. Campbell, Stephen J. Milner (Cambridge, 2004): 18–32,
especially 32.

70. For Gozzoli's work and for a recent edition of these letters, see
Diane Cole Ahl, *Benozzo Gozzoli* (New Haven, 1996), 276–277.
On Gozzoli's relationship with the Medici, see D. Kent, *Cosimo
de' Medici*, 339–341.

71. See Alison Wright, *The Pollaiuolo Brothers* (New Haven, 2005), 11–
12; Neri di Bicci, *Le Ricordanze*, 59–60, 156–157, 186, 239; Alessandro Cecchi, "Nuovi contributi sulla committenza fiorentina
di Masolino e di Masaccio," in Andrea Baldinotti, Alessandro
Cecchi e Vincenzo Farinella, *Masaccio e Masolino. Il gioco delle parti*
(Milan, 2002), 23–71; *The Brancacci Chapel: Form, Function and Setting*, ed. Nicholas Eckstein, Villa I Tatti, Harvard Center for Italian Renaissance Studies (Florence, 2007).

72. Dale V. and F. W. Kent, "Two Vignettes of Florentine Society in the Fifteenth Century," *Rinascimento* XXIII (1983): 237–260, especially 237–252, "Messer Manno Temperani and His Country Cousins."

73. David Alan Brown, *Leonardo da Vinci: Origins of a Genius* (New Haven, 1998), 47.

74. For the most extensive discussion of this work, and the argument about the new friendship between patrons and artists, see Jill Burke, *Changing Patrons: Social Identity and the Visual Arts in Renaissance Florence* (University Park, Penn., 2004); compare Patricia Zambrano and Jonathan Katz Nelson, *Filippino Lippi* (Milan, 2004), 334–335, and Jonathan Nelson, review of Burke, in *The Burlington Magazine* CXLVIII (2006): 39–40. I thank David Alan Brown for his opinion (personal communication).

75. On the importance of neighborhood ties in the *gonfalone* and parish, see D. V. and F. W. Kent, *Neighbours and Neighbourhood in Renaissance Forence: The District of the Red Lion in the Fifteenth Century* (Locust Valley, N.Y., 1982). On neighborhood as a more flexible, less institutional concept, see the papers presented by Nicholas Eckstein and Niall Atkinson to the symposium, "Human Movement in the Italian Renaissance City," at the annual meeting of the Renaissance Society of America (2007), and the symposium organized by Eckstein for 2008, "Beyond the Neighborhood: Rewriting the Italian Renaissance Community."

76. Christiane Klapisch-Zuber first drew attention to the role of *compari* (spiritual parents) in Florentine society; see her "Compérage et clientélisme à Florence (1360–1520)," *Ricerche storiche* 15 (1985): 61–76; also her analysis of the personal associations of the Niccolini family, "Parenti, amici, e vicini: il territorio urbano di una famiglia mercantile nel XV secolo," *Quaderni storici* 33 (1976): 953–982. See also Louis Haas, "'Il mio buono compare': Choosing Godparents and the Uses of Baptismal Kinship in Renaissance Florence," *Journal of Social History* 29 (1995): 341–356, especially 341 on Dati's choice of godparents for his children. On

Lorenzo's godparents, see F. W. Kent, "The Young Lorenzo 1449–1469," in *Lorenzo the Magnificent: Culture and Politics,* ed. Michale Mallett and Nicholas Mann (London, 1996), 1–22.

77. Morelli, *Ricordi,* especially 150, 195; Masi, *Ricordanze,* xviii, 6, 7, 11, 33, 42, 62.

78. MAP, XVI, 88, 5 March 1451 (1452 modern style).

79. John Kent Lydecker, *The Domestic Setting of the Arts in Renaissance Florence,* PhD diss., The Johns Hopkins University, 1988, Ann Arbor University Microfilms, 72. On the Corsini godparents, see Weissmann, *Ritual Brotherhood,* 16–19.

80. Of the godparents chosen by Medici partisans Ilarione de' Bardi and Dietisalvi Neroni, a number were fellow *amici* of the Medici, but most were neighbors. The godparents of Dietisalvi's children included poor women "per l'amore di Dio" and a wetnurse (ASF, MS 85, fols. 99r, 103r); Bardi's choices embraced a local widow and a barber "per l'amore di Dio," as well as Cosimo de' Medici's father, Giovanni di Bicci. Bardi himself was godfather to the daughter of a wool merchant who lived opposite him (ASF, Corporazioni Religiose Soppresse dal Governo Francese, ser. 119, fols. 249v, 253l, 253v).

81. Kent and Kent, *Neighbours and Neighbourhood,* 89.

82. Haas, "Il mio buono compare," 349.

83. Dante Alighieri, *The Divine Comedy, Inferno,* 19:17–18; *Paradiso,* 15:130–135.

## 3. Could Friends Be Trusted?

1. Giovanni Morelli, *Ricordi,* ed. Vittore Branca (Florence, 1956), 226.

2. For Florentine anxieties about being betrayed by friends, and some compelling examples, see Ronald F. E. Weissman, *Ritual Brotherhood in Renaissance Florence* (New York, 1982), especially chap. 2, "Judas the Florentine."

3. Archivio di stato, Florence (henceforth ASF), Mediceo avanti il

principato (henceforth MAP), II, 57. Marcus Tullius Cicero, *Laelius De Amicitia* (English and Latin), in *Old Age. On Friendship. On Divination.*, trans. W. A. Falconer (Cambridge, Mass., 1923): 103–211, 11. For Aristotle's view, articulated in his *Nichomachaean Ethics* and popularized in the fifteenth century by Matteo Palmieri, *On Civil Life*, see above, 27–28, 31.

4. Lorenzo de' Medici, *Lettere (1460–1474)* (Florence, 1977–), vol. 1, ed. Riccardo Fubini, 7–8.

5. The most detailed account of the conspiracy is that of the Medici partisan and poet Angelo Poliziano in *Della congiura dei Pazzi*, ed. Alessandro Perosa (Padua, 1958), 3–66. This is translated, with an introduction by Elizabeth Welles, as *The Pazzi Conspiracy*, in *The Earthly Republic: Italian Humanists on Government and Society*, ed. Benjamin G. Kohl and Ronald G. Witt (Philadelphia, 1978), 293–322. Piero Parenti's eyewitness account of the attempted assassination from his *Storia Fiorentina*, also included in Perosa's edition of Poliziano, 69–76, is far more balanced. Lauro Martines, *April Blood: Florence and the Plot Against the Medici* (Oxford, 2003), is the major modern study of the conspiracy, which, although blatantly anti-Medicean in its bias, provides interesting new information about the Pazzi family and their banking interests.

6. Parenti, *Storia fiorentina*, 74. On Nori's role in the Medici business, see Raymond De Roover, *The Rise and Decline of the Medici Bank* (Cambridge, Mass., 1963), passim.

7. Poliziano, *Della congiura*, 35–36. On the sacristy in which this drama was enacted, see Margaret Haines, *The "Sacrestia delle Messe" of the Florentine Cathedral* (Florence, 1983).

8. See Alison Brown, "Public Opinion and Private Interest: Lorenzo, the Monte and the Seventeen Reformers," in *Lorenzo de' Medici. Studi*, ed. Gian Carlo Garfagnini (Florence, 1992), 103–165; Alison Brown, "Uffici di onore e utile: la crisi del repubblicanesimo a Firenze," *Archivio storico italiano* CLXI (2003): 285–321.

9. See the extract from Alamanno Rinuccini, *On Liberty*, in *Human-*

*ism and Liberty: Writings on Freedom from Fifteenth-Century Florence,* ed. Renée Neu Watkins (Columbia, S.C., 1978), 49–61.

10. See Martines, *April Blood,* chap. 6.

11. *De vera amicitia: i testi del primo certame coronario,* ed. Lucia Bertolini (Modena, 1993), 291.

12. See Alison Brown, "Lorenzo and Public Opinion: The Problem of Opposition," in *Lorenzo de' Medici e il suo mondo,* ed Gian Carlo Garfagnini (Florence, 1994), 61–85; also Dale Kent, "The Dynamic of Power in Cosimo de' Medici's Florence," in *Patronage and Society in Renaissance Italy,* ed. F. W. Kent and Patricia Simons, (Oxford, 1986), 63–77.

13. On the relations between the Medici and Pazzi families in the early fifteenth century, see Dale Kent, *The Rise of the Medici: Faction in Florence 1426–1434* (Oxford, 1978), passim, especially 130, 285; on the Pazzi role in the Medici bank, see De Roover, *Rise and Decline,* passim, especially 30–31.

14. See Nicolai Rubinstein, *The Government of Florence under the Medici: 1434–1494,* 2nd ed. (Oxford, 1997) passim, and Martines, *April Blood.*

15. For the two chapels, see Howard Saalman, *Filippo Brunelleschi: The Buildings* (University Park, PA, 1993), chap. 4.

16. On the companions of Lorenzo's youth, see André Rochon, *La jeunesse de Laurent de Médicis, 1449–1478* (Paris, 1975). In 1465, Braccio Martelli married Costanza de' Pazzi. The relations between the Pazzi and the young Lorenzo are described by Martines, *April Blood,* chap. 6.

17. Poliziano, *Della congiura,* 21, 55. For the sentences of exile, 77–90.

18. On the Medici relations with the Della Stufa and the Martelli from the mid-fourteenth to the mid-fifteenth centuries, see Dale Kent, *Cosimo de' Medici and the Florentine Renaissance* (New Haven, 2000), passim, especially 179–183. On Nori's palace, see Brenda Preyer, "The 'chasa overo palagio' of Alberto di Zanobi: A Florentine Palace of About 1400 and Its Later Remodeling," Art Bulletin LXV (1983): 387–401.

19. Cicero, *De Amicitia,* 9:32–34.

20. Parenti, *Storia Fiorentina,* in Poliziano, *Della congiura,* 69.

21. ASF, MAP, V, 358, 30 April 1434.

22. For an overview of Medici, Martelli, and Della Stufa patronage at San Lorenzo, see D. Kent, *Cosimo de' Medici,* 179–197. On the friendships of the Medici and their circle with these artists, see above, chap. 2. The description of Florentines' motives for patronage is from Giovanni Rucellai, *Giovanni Rucellai ed il suo zibaldone,* ed. Alessandro Perosa (London, 1960), 121.

23. MAP, XI, 336, Cresci di Lorenzo Cresci to Cosimo de' Medici.

24. MAP, XXII, 28; XXII, 147; Isidore del Lungo, *Gli amori del magnifico Lorenzo* (Bologna, 1923), 32–59. Many similar letters to Lorenzo from members of his youthful *brigata* concerning their exploits are published by Rochon, *La jeunesse de Laurent,* chap. 2. A major study of their culture—with its intertwined elements of youth, love, and poetry (Petrarchan and Neoplatonic), as expressed in their writings, entertainments, and the art of Botticelli, which they fostered—is Charles Dempsey, *The Portrayal of Love: Botticelli's Primavera and Humanist Culture at the Time of Lorenzo the Magnificent* (Princeton, 1992).

25. Many of Lorenzo's poems relate to Lucrezia; see Dempsey, *Portrayal of Love,* chaps. 3, 4; Lorenzo de' Medici, *Canzoniere,* ed. P. Orvieto (Milan, 1984). Lorenzo's joust, in which, as it happens, he had his horse knocked out from under him by Francesco de' Pazzi, was celebrated in verse by Luigi Pulci, *Opere minori,* ed. Paolo Orvieto (Milan, 1986), 55–120; Giuliano's joust was celebrated by Angelo Poliziano, *The stanze of Angelo Poliziano (cominciate per la giostra del Magnifico Giuliano de' Medici),* trans. David Quint (Amherst, Mass., 1979). The literature on the culture of Lorenzo's circle is vast, but for the games and pleasures, and the varieties of love and friendship that it nourished, see Rochon, *La jeunesse de Laurent;* Charles Dempsey, *Portrayal of Love;* F. W. Kent, *Lorenzo de' Medici and the Art of Magnificence* (Baltimore, 2004); F. W. Kent, "The Young Lorenzo 1449–1469," in *Lorenzo*

*the Magnificent: Culture and Politics,* ed. Michael Mallett and Nicholas Mann (London, 1996): 1–22; Paola Ventrone, ed. *'Le Tems Revient': feste e spettacoli nella Firenze di Lorenzo il Magnifico* (Florence, 1992).

26. Cited by del Lungo in *Gli amori del Magnifico,* 45.

27. See Rochon, *La jeunesse de Laurent,* 132. Dempsey, *Portrayal of Love,* chap. 3.

28. See Michael Rocke, *Forbidden Friendsips: Homosexuality in Renaissance Florence* (Oxford, 1977), 198.

29. For some literal translations of Lorenzo's coded erotic poetry, see Jean Toscan, *Le carneval de langage: le lexique érotique des poètes de l'equivoque de Burchiello à Marino* (Lille, 1981), 4:1641–1656.

30. For the drawing, see Paola Barocchi, *Michelangelo e la sua scuola, I Disegni di casa Buonarroti e degli uffizi Firenze* (Florence, 1962), 253. On the Medici sculpture garden and Michelangelo, see Caroline Elam, "Il giardino delle sculture di Lorenzo de' Medici," in *Il giardino di San Marco: maestri e compagni del giovane Michelangelo,* ed. Paola Barrocchi (Florence, 1992), 157–171.

31. Michael Hirst, *Michelangelo and His Drawings* (New Haven, 1988), chap. 10, "The Making of Presents," 105; David Alan Brown and Jane Van Nimmen, *Raphael and the Beautiful Banker: The Story of the Bindo Altoviti Portrait* (New Haven, 2005), 17–29, 182n15.

32. See Marsilio Ficino, *The Letters of Marsilio Ficino* (London, 1975–), 1:61, 64; also 14, Ficino's letter to Antonio de' Pazzi; 16, his letter to Braccio Martelli.

33. Ibid., 23.

34. See Poliziano, *Stanze,* and Dempsey, *Portrayal of Love.* However, Dempsey also observes that these artistic representations gloss over tensions and undercurrents in their real relationships; see especially 145.

35. Ficino, *Letters,* 1:15.

36. For the bust and its inscription, see Lavin, "The Renaissance Bust," *Art Quarterly* 33 (1970): 214–215; also David Brown et al.,

*Virtue and Beauty: Leonardo's Ginevra de' Benci and Renaissance Portraits of Women* (Princeton, 2001), especially 162–165; on the banner, Dempsey, *Portrayal of Love*, 82–83.

37. On this drawing, see Patrizia Zambrano and Jonathan Nelson, *Filippino Lippi* (Milan, 2004), 197–201.

38. See Luke Syson, "Bertoldo di Giovanni, Republican Court Artist," in Stephen J. Campbell and Stephen Milner, eds., *Artistic Exchange and Cultural Translation in the Italian Renaissance City* (New York, 2004), 57–92. On Lorenzo's love for Bertoldo, see James Saslow, *Ganymede in the Renaissance: Homosexuality in Art and Society* (New Haven, 1986), chap. 1; F. W. Kent, "Bertoldo "sculptore" and Lorenzo de' Medici," *The Burlington Magazine* (April, 1992): 248–249.

39. For a brief account of the dramatic rift between Lorenzo and Poliziano, see Welles, introduction to Poliziano's "Conspiracy," in Kohl and Witt, *Earthly Republic.*

40. See Fubini, *Lettere*, 1:xii–xxi; Watkins, *Humanism and Liberty*, 79.

41. Paolo di Messer Pace da Certaldo, *Libro di buoni costumi*, cit. Weissman, *Ritual Brotherhood*, 40.

42. Benedetto Dei, *La Cronica dall'anno 1400 all'anno 1500*, ed. Roberto Barducci (Florence, 1985), 137–139.

43. Most of the proscriptions were published November 3, 1434, but banishments continued for some months and, indeed, periodically for the duration of the Medici regime. For the events of 1433–1434, see D. Kent, *The Rise of the Medici*, chap. 5.

44. The exile of Palla Strozzi was the one point upon which Cosimo was criticized by his otherwise laudatory biographer and friend, Vespasiano da Bisticci, *Le vite*, ed. Aulo Greco (Florence, 1970–1976), 2:164–165. On Vespasiano's other friends, see above, 128, 131–132. On Palla's last years, see Amanda Lillie, "The Memory of Place: *Luogo* and Lineage," in *Art, Memory and the Family in Renaissance Florence*, ed. Giovanni Ciappelli and Patrician Rubin (Cambridge, 2000), 195–214.

45. Cosimo de' Medici, *Ricordi,* in Angelo Fabroni, *Magni Cosmi Medicei Vita* (Pisa, 1789), 2:97–101.

46. See Phyllis Walter Gordan, *Two Renaissance Book Hunters: The Letters of Poggius Bracciolinus to Nicolaus de Niccolis* (New York, 1974), 136–137, 183. On the friendships of the Medici brothers with Poggio and Niccoli, and with Ambrogio Traversari, see D. Kent, *Cosimo de' Medici,* 23–27.

47. See Giovanni Cavalcanti, *Istorie fiorentine,* ed. G. Di Pino (Milan, 1944), 279–280.

48. Ambrogio Traversari, *Hodoeporicon,* ed. Vittorio Tamburini (Florence, 1985), 162–173.

49. Giovanni Rucellai was also a son-in-law of Palla Strozzi. He was not exiled but was declared "suspect by the state"; for his comment on this, see *Giovanni Rucellai Zibaldone,* 122. On the themes of the Brancacci chapel frescoes, see Nicholas Eckstein, ed., *The Brancacci Chapel: Form, Function and Setting,* Villa I Tatti, Harvard Center for Italian Renaissance Studies (Florence, 2007); and particularly the essay by Dale Kent, "The Brancacci Chapel Viewed in the Context of Florence's Culture," 53–71, for the collapse of the friendship between Cosimo and Felice.

50. On the feast of the chairing of Saint Peter, see Iacobus de Voragine, *The Golden Legend,* ed. and trans. William Granger Ryan (Princeton, 1993), 1:55–61. On Felice's life, see Leonida Pandimiglio, *Felice di Michele vir clarissimus e una consorteria: I Brancacci di Firenze* (Florence, 1990), especially 50, 57, 84.

51. MAP, XI, 39.

52. Ibid., XII, 409.

53. Ibid., XII, 443.

54. Ibid., C, 5.

55. For a narrative of the events of the conspiracy of 1466 and its political ramifications, see Rubinstein, *Government of Florence,* pt. 2. Margery Ganz, "Perceived Insults and their Consequences: Acciaiuoli, Neroni and Medici Relationships in the 1460s," in William J. Connell, ed. *Society and Individual in Renaissance Florence:*

*Essays in Honor of Gene A. Brucker* (Berkeley, 2002), 155–172, explores the personal affronts that contributed to the alienation of some of the conspirators; on the Soderini, see particularly Paula Clarke, *The Soderini and the Medici: Power and Patronage in Fifteenth-Century Florence* (Oxford, 1991).

56. ASF, Carte Strozziane (henceforth CS) ser. 1, 136, c. 28, 16 June 1464.
57. See especially CS ser. 1. 136, c. 29.
58. Cited by Rubinstein in *Government of Florence*, 137, Biblioteca Ambrosiana, Milan, Z 247 supra.
59. CS ser. 1, 136, c. 122.
60. Alison Brown, "Piero's Infirmity and Political Power," in *Piero de' Medici, "il Gottoso (1416–1469): Kunst im Dienste der Mediceer*, ed. Andreas Beyer and Bruce Boucher (Berlin, 1993), 9–19, suggests that Piero used his illness as a pretext for controlling the state from his bed in the Medici palace rather than consulting with his fellows in the Palace of the Priors.
61. Rubinstein, *Government of Florence*, 143.
62. Marco Parenti, *Memorie*, BNF, Magl. 272, fol. 75. See also Parenti, *Lettere*, ed. Maria Marrese (Florence, 1996), passim; see also Parenti, *Ricordi Storici (1464–1467)*, ed. Manuela Doni Garfagnini (Rome, 2001), 52–65.
63. MAP, XXII, 134.
64. MAP, II, 32, 19 February 1427 (1428 modern style).
65. Ibid., XVII, 459, 12 September 1465.
66. See Marco Parenti, *Memorie*, fols. 68r–v, 73v; also Rubinstein, *Government of Florence.*
67. This exchange is published by Fabroni, *Magni Cosmi Medicei Vita*, 2:36–37; Agnolo Acciaiuoli to Piero de' Medici, 17 September 1466, from Siena; Piero de' Medici to Agnolo Acciaiuoli, 22 September 1466, from Florence.
68. Alessandra Strozzi, *Lettere di una gentildonna fiorentinaa del secolo xv ai figliuoli esuli*, ed. Cesare Guasti (Florence, 1877), 3.
69. On Parenti and the Strozzi, see Mark Phillips, *The Memoir of*

*Marco Parenti* (Princeton, 1987); on Parenti as arbiter for the Alberti, see Brenda Preyer, "Il palazzo di messer Benedetto degli Alberti, e di Leon Battista," in *Il testamento di Leon Battista Alberti: I tempi, I lluoghi, I Protagonisti ed Enzo Bentivoglio* (Rome, 2005), 89–92.

70. Strozzi, *Lettere*, 5. On the inventory of Parenti's house, see John Kent Lydecker, *The Domestic Setting of the Arts in Renaissance Florence*, PhD diss., The Johns Hopkins University, 1988, Ann Arbor University Microfilms, 88–95.

71. On this gift, see D. Kent, *Cosimo de' Medici*, 108–110.

72. Parenti, *Lettere*, 46–49.

73. Niccolò Machiavelli, *Lettere*, ed. F. Gaeta (Milan, 1961), 6:303; see also John M. Najemy, *Between Friends: Discourses of Power and Desire in the Machiavelli-Vettori Letters of 1513–1515* (Princeton, 1993), 236.

74. See Joseph Tusiani, *The Complete Poems of Michelangelo* (New York, 1960), 43–44. On the drawings Michelangelo made for his friends, see Hirst, *Michelangelo and his Drawings*, chap. 10. Vasari listed four presentation drawings that Michelangelo gave to Tommaso Cavalieri, one of them being a *Rape of Ganymede*. Figure 3.12 is not this drawing, now lost, but it is thought to be very similar to the original and probably by Michelangelo.

75. For the sonnets, see Tusiani, *Complete Poems*, 114, 152. For the correspondence between Michelangelo and Colonna, and the drawings and poems he dedicated to her, see Monica Bianco and Vittoria Romani, "Vittoria Colonna e Michelangelo," in *Vittoria Colonna e Michelangelo*, ed. Pina Ragionieri, (Florence, 2005), 145–191.

# Index

# Index

# Index

# Index

# Index

# Index

# Index

# Index

# Index